RISK IQ

**Risk Management Fundamentals
For Business and Personal Life**

First Edition

What's Your Risk IQ?

Amy Arp, Ph.D.

Copyright © 2017 by Amy Arp

All rights reserved. Unless otherwise indicated, all materials on these pages are copyrighted. No part of these pages, either text or image may be used for any purpose other than personal use. Therefore, reproduction, modification, storage in a retrieval system or retransmission, in any form or by any means, electronic, mechanical or otherwise, for reasons other than personal use, is strictly prohibited without prior written permission from the author or publisher.

All trademarks are the property of their respective companies.

Catalog-in-Publication Data is on file with the Library of Congress.

ISBN-13: 978-1974667239

Printed in the United States of America

ACKNOWLEDGMENTS

First and always, I thank God for all good things. Without Him I am truly nothing. I would also like to thank Bobbie Duke for all the editing help; you are one in a million. Amy Bray, my life coach, thank you for making me believe that I can do anything. And to all those who have played a part in making this book a reality, both through encouragement to take the risk and through expertise, thank you from the bottom of my heart.

TABLE OF CONTENTS

Introduction	1
1 Risk Overview	3
2 The Science of Risk	13
3 Risk IQ	25
→ Risk IQ Test #1	28
4 Risk Personalities	35
5 Risk Profile	47
6 Silent Risks	59
7 Total Cost of Risk	69
8 Commercial Risk	81
9 Staying Power	103
10 Famous Risk Takers	111
11 The Laws of Risk-Taking	117
→ Risk IQ Test #2	129
Appendix A: Questions to ponder	135
Appendix B: Insurance Terms	141
Appendix C: Risk Tolerance Study	153
About the Author	169

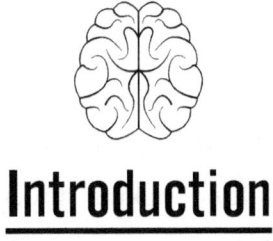

Introduction

As a young child, I got a wonderful first-hand introduction to the wide array of risk-tolerant personalities. In fact, the story starts the day I was born when I had no comprehension of the concept of risk or much of anything else for that matter.

As I was coming into the world, one of my father's first fears about my well-being was the chance of me drowning in our backyard in-ground swimming pool. In his zest to protect me, he planned to fill the pool with sand, removing that risk factor altogether. Luckily, my mother took a different slant and made him put his shovel away.

While the swimming pool incident made for a funny story growing up, it was a very clear picture of my father's approach to risk. He avoided it at all costs. The uncertainty of life made him nervous and he did everything in his power to control the risk.

My mother, on the other hand, is a risk seeker of sorts. She loves the thrill of risk-filled activities. In my not so wildest dreams, I could even envision her swimming with the sharks off the coast of Hawaii or running with the bulls in Pamplona. Needless to say, I had some interesting moments growing up watching them work out their differing opinions and approaches to risk.

Observing the extreme positions of the risk tolerance spectrum represented by my dad on one side and my mother on the other gave me a perspective of risk awareness that awakened my curiosity. What could cause such drastic differences between two people so dear to me?

Risk is everywhere. From walking down the street to making a decision to start a new venture, it is an unavoidable certainty that surrounds every aspect of our lives. To some, risk-taking has the makings of a welcome adventure. To others it may sound like a horror movie. We all have unique approaches to risk.

Over the years, I have learned that risk is somewhat of a game. Some win and some lose. As a Commercial Risk Manager, I continually encounter business owners who approach risk differently. Some want to purchase insurance to cover any situation that could possibly arise, and others want to find the cheapest policy possible. I have observed tendencies and strategies along the way that differentiate the winners from the losers.

Risk, by its very definition, involves uncertainty. You can, however, learn how to control and manage risk in a way that will increase your chances for success. And by that I do not mean solely purchasing insurance, which is the obvious tactic. Insurance is one of the ways to mitigate risk, but it is only one aspect of risk mitigation.

The first step in improving your chances of winning at the risks you take is to understand your individual approach to risk, which I call your "Risk IQ." After you determine your Risk IQ, you can learn what you can control to give yourself an edge that will improve your chances for success.

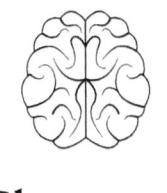

Chapter 1

RISK OVERVIEW

"Twenty years from now you will be more disappointed by the things you didn't do than by the ones you did. So throw off the bowlines, sail away from the safe harbor, catch the trade winds in your sails. Explore. Dream. Discover."

—Mark Twain

Risk is everywhere. We are confronted with it on a daily or even hourly basis. Regardless if you are an individual managing the risks you face in your personal life or if you are responsible for a business which also faces risks, risk management is a skill you must learn and implement. And I applaud you for taking the time to invest in this skill by reading this book.

The primary focuses of this book include risk management and understanding your unique risk personality. To do this, we will go through a general overview of risk to lay the groundwork for some of the more advanced principles. You may find some areas with which you are already familiar, but stick with me because the goal is building to some of the more advanced concepts.

What Is A Risk IQ?

Risk IQ is an assessment that was created to help you in your risk management journey. Risk IQ is much more simplified than the vanilla mental IQ. Risk IQ is based off your knowledge about risk related definitions and approaches and your ability to implement those strategies. When you get to chapter 3, you will be given a pre-test to determine your Risk IQ. At the book's completion, you will be given a post-test to see your improvement. You then can go back and review any needed areas.

Do You Have What it Takes?

As an entrepreneur, I am frequently approached with business ideas and concepts and asked if I think they will be successful or not. I have heard both good ideas and poor ideas, but an idea alone is not enough to base a prediction of success or failure.

A good friend of mine, I will call her Kate, once excitedly told me about a spa she wanted to open. At the time I owned a medical day spa, and she wanted to hear my thoughts on her unique concept. She shared her ideas and, I must admit, she had a fantastic concept and had a location picked out that was perfect. I wanted to recommend and fully encourage her to swing for the fences, but I couldn't. I know Kate, her strengths and weaknesses and her general approach to life.

I know that Kate hates risk. She has always wanted success that appeared to be a serious stretch, but her fear of failure has kept her from fully attempting a new venture. I cautioned her to really identify and calculate the estimated costs. While I thought the spa venture was a great idea, there would inevitably be bumps in the road that would challenge her progress.

She went forward with her idea and started with a bang. Six months after she opened, she encountered some challenges and sold the business at a loss. Kate lamented ever taking the risk. The business went on to be a smashing success under the new owner, and is still open now, ten years later. Kate didn't fully understand risk. She didn't understand her appetite for it, and she didn't have a solid plan for managing the risk.

From the budding entrepreneur to the most seasoned CEO, everyone has a level of risk they are comfortable with taking. This comfort level affects your strategy and your ability to stay in the game when things get tough.

Much of the discomfort comes from fear of the unknown; this book is designed to help you determine your tolerance for risk and to demystify the process. You have more control than you think, and risk is less a game of chance than it initially appears.

Defining Risk

In order to make sure we are speaking the same language regarding risk and risk management, I am going to take some time to introduce various topics related to risk, each of which I will expound upon further in subsequent chapters.

According to the dictionary, risk as a noun is defined as "exposure to the chance of injury or loss; a hazard or dangerous chance." As a verb, it means willingly engaging in that activity in light of that exposure.

> **risk** [risk] *noun*
>
> **Definition of** RISK
>
> 1 : possibility of loss or injury : PERIL
>
> 2 : someone or something that creates or suggests a hazard
>
> 3 a : the chance of loss or the perils to the subject matter of an insurance contract; *also* : the degree of probability of such loss
> b : a person or thing that is a specified hazard to an insurer
> c : an insurance hazard from a specified cause or source • war *risk*
>
> 4 : the chance that an investment (such as a stock or commodity) will lose value

It's no surprise to anyone that life is made up of risks. While the above definition is quite broad, the subject itself covers an incredibly varied spectrum of possibilities. Soldiers risk life and limb when going into battle. Children risk ridicule when they raise their hand in the classroom if they don't have the correct answer. Shoppers risk selecting the wrong product when they pick something off a shelf. Risk is everywhere.

It's not the presence or absence of risk that is at issue, it's what we decide to do about it each time we encounter risk—and most of us encounter it many times during the course of each day. It all boils down to choices. Do we decide to take a risk, or do we decide to avoid it? Is it truly up to chance, or do we have some measure of control?

Risk Tolerance

People's unique reaction to risk leads to the subject of risk tolerance. When it comes to making important decisions, whether they be pivotal personal choices or strategic business decisions, the level of risk tolerance with which we are comfortable is a primary driver.

The term risk tolerance is used primarily in business, mostly in the world of financial investing. The term has a wider application; so I use it to encompass activities and decisions in day-to-day living.

One real life example is the choice each of us makes when driving to and from work each day. Do you drive in the slow lane or the fast lane? How fast do you drive with regard to the speed limit? Something as simple as our driving habits is a very telling indicator of our propensity for risk.

Risk Management — Risk Assessment

Not unlike risk tolerance, the term risk management is in effect owned by the business domain. Under my larger risk perspective umbrella however, I'm applying the risk management mentality to our everyday existence.

Going back to my trusty dictionary, the term risk management refers to the process of determining the maximum acceptable level of overall risk a person or business is willing to accept with regard to a given activity. An essential component of risk management is risk assessment and the two are inseparable.

Risk assessment techniques are used to determine the initial level of perceived risk associated with the activity being contemplated. If that risk seems excessive, one must then develop a plan to reduce the amount of risk to an acceptable level. Keep in mind that large activities such as relocating to a new city or starting a new business venture involve many sub-activities each having their own risk factors.

With risk management and risk assessment I'll take a big picture look at both the individual components and the entire project simultaneously. From an overall standpoint, risk management is the process of evaluating the chance of loss or damage of any kind and subsequently taking steps to reduce or eliminate the pending risk.

Lending money is an example of risk management we can all easily understand. Whether you're a bank, a mortgage company, a car dealership or even an individual considering extending a personal loan, you engage in risk management or at least risk assessment. As you perform your due diligence prior to making the loan, you naturally determine the chances the borrower may not pay you back.

If you sense the chances of having the loan not repaid are significant, you may decide not to make the loan at all or you may charge a higher interest rate to cover the higher risk. Or you may ask the borrower to pledge collateral to secure the loan. Checking a person's credit score and/or credit references should be an essential part of the risk assessment.

From a consumer standpoint, we are almost always presented with a risk management opportunity when we make certain purchases. When we purchase items such as electronic devices or household appliances, are we not offered an extended warranty for an additional fee? Guess what? That's risk management at the personal level.

The Cost of Risks

What does risk actually cost? Unfortunately, that's usually one of life's mysteries. In the majority of cases, it's a number that defies calculation. There are some simple risks for which the cost is easily calculated. When buying a lottery ticket for instance, you're only risking the price of the ticket…like maybe one to five dollars.

So, let's look at the two basic categories of risk, speculative risk and pure risk.

With speculative risk, there are three possible results. First, nothing may happen, in which case the result is breaking even. The other two are polar opposites. The result may be good, which means you've won, or it may be bad, which means you lose.

Gambling and investing in stocks and bonds are examples of speculative risks. These offer the chance of making money, losing money or staying even.

There is no insurance available on the traditional insurance market for speculative risk. Placing "hedge bets" is the only realistic way to reduce the risk exposure when investing. Strategies for this are actions such as portfolio diversification or purchasing derivatives.

With pure risk, also known as absolute risk, there are only two possible outcomes: either something bad will happen or nothing will happen. Insurance is readily available to guard against major losses from negative results in pure risk situations. One can buy car insurance to cover the cost of accidents or home owner's insurance to pay for fire damage and things of that nature. For a price, insurance companies will allow us to insure almost anything from the mundane to the absurd. Lloyds of London specializes in the latter.

Insurance companies employ mathematical experts such as actuaries to calculate the odds of bad things happening. Let's face it, just being alive involves risk. All sorts of maladies are lurking in the darkness just waiting for us to screw up or become unlucky.

It's up to those experts at the insurance companies to calculate two things: 1) the odds of particular bad things happening to us, and 2) the cost of repairing the damage caused when they do happen. In addition, actuaries are involved in calculating—on average—when individuals are likely to meet their demise. They then combine those three factors to determine the premium we must pay to protect ourselves from monetary loss.

Personal Risk vs. Business Risk

At the personal level, the calculation of risk costs seems rather straightforward but there are myriad hidden complexities. In looking at just a few of the considerations insurance companies must factor into their formulas, we can see this is no easy task. The data that is needed to make the calculations is staggering.

- How does a person's health history factor into projected illness-related expenses?

- What effect does someone's lifestyle have on their projected longevity?

- How does the neighborhood in which a person lives affect the odds of bad things happening to them or their property?

- Which occupations carry the highest risk of work-related injuries?

……this list could go on for many more pages.

Stepping into the business world, matters get far more complicated. Total cost of risk for a business is the sum of all aspects of its operations that relate to risk. The risk of incurring a loss instead of earning a profit is the most visible, but it's only the tip of the iceberg.

In large corporations, the cost of controlling risk with the deployment of expensive risk management programs and departments can have a major impact on the company's bottom line. By the same token, a company may be taking a serious chance of being forced out of business if they don't spend enough on risk management.

Intangible Costs

While the costs of speculative and pure risks can often be calculated with surprising accuracy, there are countless risks we take on a regular and even ongoing basis where putting a price tag on them is virtually impossible.

- What is the cost of not taking care of our health?
- What is the cost of a failed marriage…beyond just the attorney fees?
- What is the true cost of being busted for driving under the influence?
- What is the cost of emotional trauma?
- What is the cost of a severely damaged reputation?
- What is the cost of failing to back up the hard drive on your personal computer?

  …I'll stop here before I scare you any further.

In Conclusion

Risk is an uncertainty that has aspects that can be controlled. It will never be fully controlled, even with the best risk management program available. There are two elements I will be focusing on in the remaining chapters: your personal risk tolerance profile and ways to develop a strategic approach to risk that will provide the greatest chances of success.

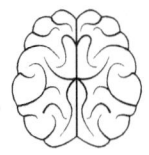

Chapter 2

THE SCIENCE OF RISK

> *"Nothing in life is to be feared, it is only to be understood. Now is the time to understand more, so that we may fear less."*
>
> — **Marie Curie**

When brain science is mentioned, most people immediately think of the right brain vs. left brain scenario. Risk is neither a right-brain nor left-brain phenomenon — it's more a front and back proposition. I'll talk more about the frontal lobe in a minute.

Are people who are labeled as risk-takers wired differently? That's a burning question for which researchers and scientists have been searching for answers over the past several decades.

One of the best ways to find answers to this question is by studying the chemistry of the brain. In the early 1990s, researchers in Israel identified what they believed to be the "risk gene." Subsequent research further identified this as the DRD4 gene.

Before I get into the discussion of this supposed risk gene, I need to provide the proper context by explaining a little about the makeup of the brain itself. Relax, this is not going to be a lengthy dissertation on the chemical makeup of the brain.

So, here comes the *Cliff Notes* version:

For simplicity, let's look at the three components of the brain that most affect risk-taking:

Basal Ganglia — This is the pleasure center courtyard of the brain. It understands the finer things in life such as food, money, sex and other pleasurable things that make us happy. It guides our social behavior, craves instant gratification and promotes impulsive behavior in search of positive rewards. Ever the optimist, it leads to fast-thinking and going for the gusto.

Prefrontal Cortex (PFC) — This is like the central processing unit (CPU) of a computer. It accepts input from the basal ganglia and other sources and processes them according to our learned set of rules and regulations. The PFC tempers the enthusiasm of the basal ganglia by incorporating common sense, reasoning, judgment, self-control, inhibition, rationality and other down-to-earth reality enforcements. It is the command center of the brain's frontal lobe — the largest part of the brain and the thing that differentiates humans from lower-order species.

Limbic System—If the PFC is the brain's CPU, the limbic system is its hard drive. It's where our emotion and memories are stored. It brings our learned experience and emotions to bear on decision-making. It's our built-in fight or flight responder.

The basal ganglia and PFC are tightly coupled with neural connectors. They communicate closely with each other and collaborate with the limbic system to determine optimal actions for us to take. If our brain was an automobile, the basal ganglia would be the gas pedal and the PFC would be the brakes.

These three sections working together make up our internal probability calculator we use for risk assessment and decision-making. It's also where learning takes place. Scientists agree that making risky decisions is mental exercise for the brain—over time, it makes us learn faster and more efficiently.

Now that we have the city center of our brain identified and have its two prominent suburbs outlined, let's examine the roadway infrastructure that supports traffic moving throughout our cranial community.

The scientific term for the primary freeway that allows thoughts, emotions and such to travel freely between the sectors of the brain is the mesocortical pathway. It is essential to the normal cognitive function of the prefrontal cortex and is thought to be involved in cognitive control, motivation, and emotional response.

This mesocortical pathway is only one of the four major pathways in the brain. Don't worry if you're not grasping all the scientific jargon. Just think of the brain as a central city with its suburbs and roadway system that allows sensations to traverse through its various communities.

Is Dopamine What Makes Us Dopes?

Now that we have part of our brain's thoroughfare infrastructure laid out, let's look at the vehicular traffic that's running around inside our heads.

Brace yourself because here comes another one of those academic scientific terms. The cars and buses traveling around in our brains are called neurotransmitters. On the subject of the risk gene, we can envision dopamine as the Amtrak Train behemoth of all neurotransmitters. According to scientists, dopamine is linked to many neurological and psychiatric conditions including ADHD, addictive behaviors and even schizophrenia and bipolar disorder.

The risk gene, or DRD4 receptor mentioned above is activated by the dopamine traveling through the metropolitan sectors of our brain. This is what makes it easier for people to respond to stress or anxiety. The higher your threshold for those feelings, the higher your tolerance for risk. The higher your level of absorbed dopamine, the greater chance you have of being a thrill-seeking risk-taker.

Higher levels of dopamine lead to impulsivity and novelty-seeking. This makes sense since researchers have found people who are prone to risk-taking tend to be more exploratory than average. An article in Elite Daily even referred to dopamine in conjunction with DRD4 as the "wanderlust gene," claiming that people with high levels of it "are just born to be travelers."

So where does dopamine come from in the first place? Studies have shown that people who eat meat and fish have higher dopamine levels than those who don't. Interesting! Can we infer from this that vegetarians tend

> "Can we infer that vegetarians tend not to be risk-takers?"

not to be risk-takers? Thinking about the people I know who are vegetarians, that thought seems to have merit. But before jumping to that conclusion, let's consider the cause and effect correlation.

Perhaps vegetarians avoid eating meat due to the opinion held by some that meat-eaters run a higher risk of heart disease and fish-eaters may be plagued with mercury poisoning. So, we may have the familiar chicken and egg conundrum at work here.

A University of Delaware study suggested that another neurotransmitter, serotonin, plays a role in risk-taking tendencies as well. This chemical helps inhibit impulsive behavior, and it could be in short supply in people who take chances.

More Pieces to the Puzzle

Researchers agree that taking sizeable risks releases adrenaline in our body. This gives us that quick rush of excitement. Couple that with the increased flow of dopamine, which causes intense feelings of pleasure, and we can see why some people get enjoyment from taking risks. This powerful high can be addictive in many cases.

Over time, conditioning plays a major role in the risk/reward game as well as the chemicals themselves. Risk-takers may need bigger and bigger risks to get the same rush, and mundane daily activities can start to be boring. This is due to the fact that a person's expectations come into play. When a positive result is unexpected, the amount of adrenaline and dopamine released is higher than if the same result is expected.

When a thrill-seeker gets that exhilarating rush, he or she wants to repeat the activity to feel the same rush again. But the brain plays a little trick on us. In skydiving, the second parachute jump will not have quite the same effect as the first because the brain now knows what to expect. And by the 100th jump...well, it's just a walk in the park. This is what causes the extreme risk-takers to keep taking chances that are progressively more dangerous.

Now let's take a look at the flip side of the dopamine coin. It's not all about rewards. When a person has a bad thing happen, it's more like a punishment than a reward. With negative experiences, dopamine does not get released. While we're not necessarily feeling pain, we're not getting pleasure either. Therefore we have no desire to repeat the experience.

Looking at the bigger picture, the risk-taking game is not just about science. Gender and age also come into play.

Researchers generally agree that males tend to be more prone to risk-taking than females. Some attribute this to higher levels of testosterone in men while others say it has more to do with societal influences, so the jury is still out on that issue. Most researchers have found age to be a strong determinant of risk propensity. As we age, our willingness to take risks decreases naturally.

Our Built-in Risk Calculator

Now that our brief science lesson is over — thank God — I'll get back to the fun stuff.

The various physical components of the brain working in concert with dopamine and probably a few other gene-related neurotransmitters make up our very own, highly-personalized risk calculator.

As part of our day-to-day lives, we routinely evaluate the relative risks and rewards associated with the various options presented to us every day. While some of these evaluations involve a great deal of thought and sometimes even anguish, many have become somewhat automatic. Our subconscious mind performs more risk evaluations than we can imagine.

Both in our personal lives and in business activities, we are constantly making decisions that involve risks of all varieties. In our personal lives we make choices that affect our level of comfort, our social standing and many other intangible aspects of our existence. In business, we may select options that are potentially more profitable than others while understanding the alternatives may offer a safer path along with the more modest rewards.

Our brain-resident risk calculator is the key contributor to these constant decision making processes. Figuring out the odds of success vs. failure and the probable values of certain vs. uncertain rewards keeps our brain busy all day long. I think it's safe to say this does not stop even after we go to sleep at night. While our body is sound asleep in bed, our brain is still working on its constant job of making risk-reward calculations.

We must understand that it's not all about mathematical formulas. Our internal risk calculator is also fueled by our intuition. Our brain balances input from emotional and memory centers of the cortex combining tangible and intangible reasoning.

While we understand that probabilities can be calculated, most risks are truly undertaken without knowing the actual probabilities. Risk is a calculation but a very complicated, multi-faceted one, and the result is not always rational.

The Psychology of Risk

Knowing what we know about neurotransmitters and risk/reward calculations, there's still at least one more dimension to consider. Our emotions play a huge role in the risk-taking dramatization.

All of us have friends and acquaintances who fall under the category of adrenaline junkies, you know those kind of crazy folks who go sky-diving, whitewater kayaking or helicopter skiing.

Personality plays a major role in an individual's penchant for risky behavior. An individual with a flamboyant persona is far more likely to take up hang-gliding than one with a sedate temperament. Whether it's their fun-loving nature or propensity for showing off how fearless they are, the participant's frame of mind alone can lead to edgy behavior.

> "Personality plays a major role in an individual's penchant for risky behavior."

While we all know these adrenaline seekers, we also know people who are obvious worry-warts. While logic tells us those who are excessively worriers don't make good candidates for risk-taking, some studies indicate that people who score high on neuroticism—a combination of anxiety, moodiness, and worry—are actually quite likely to become thrill-seekers. It could be their inner selves crying to break out of the mold that pushes them toward the edge.

Certain habits that form can also affect the kinds of risks a person is willing to take. The serious cigarette smoker might be terrified by the thought of jumping out of an airplane with a parachute without ever recognizing that smoking might be an even riskier behavior.

People whose makeup includes a flair for novelty might travel to dangerous locations just to experience something new in their lives.

The Risk Gap

A study published a few years ago in the Journal of Experimental Psychology involved a concept the researchers called the "risk gap," the differentiation between our own appetite for taking certain risks and what risks we might suggest others take.

Head researcher Sarah Helfinstein of the University of Maryland pointed out that people use different standards based on whether they are considering a given risk for themselves or advocating it for a friend or acquaintance.

On the surface, one might assume that almost everyone would be more likely to recommend risky behaviors to others than to take the same risks themselves. Such is not always the case. Many people with a propensity for risk-taking realize they flirt with danger more often and to a greater degree than what others would consider to be acceptable. They will accordingly back away from encouraging others to take risks at the same level.

How We Take Risks

The manner in which we put ourselves "in gear" to take a risk varies significantly from person to person and from one situation to another.

Some get inspired to take a risk because they learned about someone who reaped a great reward by taking a certain risk. Perhaps a friend bet a week's pay at the craps table in Las Vegas and walked away with a huge bundle of cash. Wow, if it worked for them, it might work for me.

Others may feel they are forced into taking a risk out of desperation. Let's stick with the Las Vegas theme and look at someone facing foreclosure on their home. They may see their only way out is to make some hefty bets with 35-to-1 odds at the roulette wheel in the hopes of catching up on their delinquent mortgage payments.

Those of us on the sidelines see this as sheer folly, but the better feels this 'all or nothing' gamble is worth it because the thought of being homeless is simply too overwhelming to handle.

An acquaintance of mine who lives on the West Coast had run a successful construction business for over 20 years before the housing market collapsed in 2008-2010. With his source of income virtually dried up and job opportunities looking bleak, his savings were dwindling at warp speed.

During his frantic job search, he stumbled into an opportunity to become a construction manager with an overseas contracting firm. The bad news is that the position was in war-torn Afghanistan where terrorist activity was rampant. His job sites would be targets for rocket attacks, mortar fire and sniper activity.

After several days of agonizing over the decision, he and his wife came to the conclusion that he should take the job. While his construction buddies in the U.S. were filing for bankruptcy, he got his affairs in order and headed off to the Middle East.

The guy spent a hair-raising four years in Afghanistan suffering deplorable living conditions and dodging terrorist bullets while supervising construction jobs. He finally returned home with a re-invigorated bank account and no serious injuries. The risk paid off, but could easily have gone in the opposite direction.

Most of us like to believe we only take big chances after we have carefully calculated the risk/reward factor involved. Here's where that cranial risk calculator mentioned earlier comes into play.

Our memory bank searches through our brain-resident archives to evaluate past experiences, whether they be personal ones or those of friends and associates. We weigh the odds of future outcomes occurring based on historical results given similar situations.

Most of us resort to performing due diligence of varying degrees by gathering pertinent information and/or expert opinions. We weigh the pros and cons before deciding whether or not to take on certain risks.

And for many, it just comes down to good old gut feel.

Our social environment and the company we keep also plays an important role in risk-taking and the related decision making. Friends, family and business associates can be powerful influencers.

Researchers have repeatedly found we are far more likely to take a particular risk ourselves if we know someone else who has taken the same risk, even if it involves an outcome that's potentially harmful. And it does not mean the other person's outcome had to be a stellar success.

Perhaps it was just a matter of them living to tell about it. Having a friend survive a death-defying experience like skydiving may lead us to dispense with the "what's the worst that can happen" question.

So What Does This All Mean?

Due to the power of our brain chemistry and its storage capability, we're somewhat limited on how much control we have over our basic instincts where risk tolerance is concerned.

There are, however, a few things we can do to improve our appetite for risk if we desire to do so. Some scientists believe that increasing the amount of meat and fish in our diet will help some. However, there is limited proof of that and there is no quantitative data to support it.

> "There are a few things we can do to improve our appetite for risk."

The primary avenue we have for changing our risk appetite is to step out of our comfort zone and actually take some risks we would not otherwise take. To be on the safe side, one should not go wild with this scenario. Start slow and build up as you feel safe to do so.

As you take new risks and hopefully have positive results, the pride and satisfaction you feel will be stored in your limbic system, your memory bank.

From that point on, your internal risk calculator will probably be more receptive to risk taking.

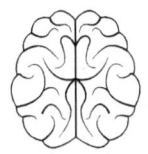

Chapter 3

RISK IQ

"It is not that I'm so smart. But I stay with the questions much longer."

—**Albert Einstein**

Risk plays a vital role in our strategy and decision-making. While we can't all be risk management professionals, we should take the time to examine our personal approach to risk and become educated on how to manage the risks we do face.

Before I get into Risk IQ, I'd like to set the table by making sure we're on the same page with regard to IQ itself. Intelligence Quotient is the measure of a person's cognitive capacity relative to his or her peers. It is computed by dividing the person's mental age (as measured on a scale such as Stanford-Binet Scale) by his or her chronological age, and multiplying by 100. Measuring IQ is different than measuring achievement. Achievement is the result of effort; intelligence is related to aptitude.

I think we can all agree that some very intelligent people with high IQs have done some pretty stupid things in certain situations because intelligence does not correlate directly to common sense. Whereas IQ tends to be based on your aptitude, *Risk IQ is based on your knowledge*. It is much easier to increase knowledge than it is to improve aptitude. Intelligence plays an important role in Risk IQ due to the need to rationalize many, often diverse, factors simultaneously.

Unlike a regular IQ, a Risk IQ is not a single fixed number that defines your intelligence level. A low Risk IQ doesn't mean you are stupid and a high Risk IQ doesn't mean you are smart. It only describes what you have been exposed to, retained and implemented. It is also worth noting that your Risk IQ does not correlate to your tolerance for risk. Your Risk Personality type, which will be covered in a future chapter, will help you understand your unique pre-dispositions towards risk.

How Does Knowing your Risk IQ Help?

We live in an information based economy in which success is largely dependent on its human resources. As society progresses, specialization continues. We hone our skills to be more strategic. Because risk plays such a vital role in the course of our lives and businesses, it makes sense to take some time and improve our understanding of risk.

With the possible exception of taking "miracle drugs" — if there are such things — there is little we can do to change our IQ…we're basically stuck with what God gave us. Changing our Risk IQ, however, is easily done with research and careful implementation.

I work in the insurance world, but I want to let you in on a little secret: before I was an insurance agent, I don't think I read one policy in full during all my years in business before I worked in insurance. It can be complex and I didn't know what to look for. Knowing what I know now, I understand how important it is to know what to look for. And I would absolutely take on the role of risk manager much more deliberately. Risk is something you can manage, but it takes effort.

Your personal and business Risk IQs as calculated in the test below will highlight the aspects of risk awareness where your knowledge may need to be expanded. Please remember that this book is meant to be a basic overview of risk. Depending on your needs and specialization, you may need to dig deeper.

This book helps you gain a working knowledge of the topics and makes you a more informed risk taker. It will also show you where you may need to consult other professionals in the risk management process. This book is by no means meant to be a form of legal advice in the area of risk management.

Presented first is the Personal Risk IQ, followed by the Business Risk IQ for company owners and professionals managing corporate risk.

THE RISK IQ TEST

For each of the questions below, simply mark a YES or NO. At the bottom, you'll simply tally up the YES column and the NO column and plug those numbers into the simple formula provided.

PERSONAL RISK IQ

Risk Basics

- Y N - I understand the definition for risk management.
- Y N - I understand what a risk assessment is.
- Y N - I understand what a vulnerability is.
- Y N - I understand what probability is.
- Y N - I understand what impact is.
- Y N - I understand what compensating controls are.
- Y N - I understand what an inherent risk is.
- Y N - I understand what a residual risk is.
- Y N - I understand how to weigh the pros and cons of a risk-based decision.
- Y N - I understand the difference between and benefits of retaining, avoiding, reducing and transferring a risk.
- Y N - I understand Total Cost of Risk.
- Y N - I understand what property insurance is.
- Y N - I understand what liability insurance is.

Y N - I understand what a declarations page is.

Y N - I understand what an exclusion is.

Y N - I understand what an endorsement is.

Y N - I understand the difference between "named perils" and "specific perils".

Personal Risks

Y N - I have performed a personal risk assessment on my life.

Y N - I understand health insurance and have made an informed decision on how to proceed.

Y N - I understand ancillary insurances (dental, vision) and have made an informed decision on how to proceed.

Y N - I understand home insurance/rental insurance and have made an informed decision on how to proceed.

Y N - I understand personal liability insurance and have made an informed decision on how to proceed.

Y N - I have performed a housing vulnerability check and implemented necessary changes.

Y N - I have performed a vehicular vulnerability check and implemented necessary changes.

Y N - I understand risks I encounter while traveling and implement the necessary precautions when necessary.

Y N - I understand cyber risks and have implemented the necessary precautions/protections.

Financial Risks

Y N - I have three months of savings in the bank in case of an emergency.

Y N - I have a retirement account set up.

Y N - I understand identity protection and have made an informed decision on how to proceed.

Y N - I understand what ransomware is and steps I can take to protect myself.

End of Life Risks

Y N - I understand and have evaluated life insurance and have made an informed decision on how to proceed.

Y N - I have created a last will and testament.

End of Personal Risk IQ test

Risk IQ Formula

- Count the number of YES answers and the number of NO answers.

- Divide the number of No answers by the number of YES answers.

- Multiply that number by 100.

- Your answer will be between 1 and 100, with 100 being a perfect score.

Your Personal Risk IQ Score _____

BUSINESS RISK IQ

Risk Basics

Y N - I understand the definition of risk management.

Y N - I understand what a risk assessment is.

Y N - I understand what a vulnerability is.

Y N - I understand what probability is.

Y N - I understand what impact is.

Y N - I understand what compensating controls are.

Y N - I understand what an inherent risk is.

Y N - I understand what a residual risk is.

Y N - I understand how to weigh the pros and cons of a risk-based decision.

Y N - I understand Total Cost of Risk.

Y N - I understand the difference between and benefits of retaining, avoiding, reducing and transferring a risk.

Y N - I understand what liability insurance is.

Y N - I understand what a declarations page is.

Y N - I understand what an exclusion is.

Y N - I understand what an endorsement is.

Y N - I understand the difference between "named perils" and "specific perils."

Y N - I understand a workers compensation policy and how I can control the costs.

Y N - I understand what crime insurance is.

Y N - I understand what errors and omissions insurance is.

Y N - I understand what directors' and officers' liability insurance is.

Y N - I understand property insurance.

Y N - I understand liability insurance.

Y N - I understand what health insurance options I have for my company.

Y N - I understand Business Interruption Insurance and Contingent Business Interruption Insurance.

Commercial Risks

Y N - I have performed a commercial risk assessment on my business.

Y N - I have made an informed choice about choosing an insurance broker.

Y N - I have performed a safety audit at my place of business.

Y N - I have performed a vehicular vulnerability check and implemented necessary safeguards.

Y N - I have created and implemented a business continuity plan for my place of business.

Y N - I understand cyber risks and have implemented the necessary precautions/protections.

Y N - I understand active shooter risks and have made a plan for my place of business.

Y N - I have researched the best available safety equipment and have made an informed decision on how to proceed.

Y N - I have contacted a disaster recovery company and have established a relationship that will guarantee services within 24 hours in the case of an emergency.

Y N - I implement employee trainings on a regular basis.

Y N - I have policies in place to back up data on a regular basis.

Business Continuation Risks

Y N - I understand what a business continuity plan is.

Y N - I understand and have evaluated life insurance and have made an informed decision on how to proceed.

Y N - I have created a last will and testament that clearly outlines my instructions for my company in the event of my death or incapacitation.

Y N - I have evaluated a buy-sell agreement or key man insurance policy.

End of Business Risk IQ test

Risk IQ Formula

- Count the number of YES answers and the number of NO answers.

- Divide the number of No answers by the number of YES answers.

- Multiply that number by 100.

- Your answer will be between 1 and 100, with 100 being a perfect score.

Your Business Risk IQ Score _____

These two Risk IQ scores and the individual answers should give you a guide to the subjects on which you probably want to do more studying to be a more informed person with regard to risk taking and risk management.

Remember, while your traditional IQ may be more of a static number, your Risk IQ was intended to be raised. It can be a guide to work through to understand your risk management knowledge and implementation. It may not be today, and it may not be tomorrow, but by continuing to grow in your understanding and ability to implement these topics you will be on your way to having an effective risk management program.

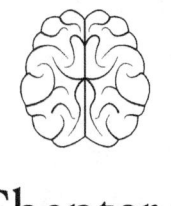

Chapter 4

RISK PERSONALITIES

"Positive expectations are the mark of the superior personality."
— **Brian Tracy**

When I was a young child, I got a wonderful first-hand introduction to the wide array of risk-tolerant personalities. In fact, the story starts the day I was born when I had no comprehension of the concept of risk or much of anything else for that matter.

As I was coming into the world, one of my father's first fears about my well-being was the chance of me drowning in our backyard in-ground swimming pool. In his zest to protect me, he planned to fill the pool with sand, removing that risk factor altogether. Luckily, my mother took a different slant and made him put his shovel away.

While the swimming pool incident made for a funny story growing up, it was a very clear picture of my father's approach to risk. He avoided it at all costs. The uncertainty of life made him nervous and he did everything in his power to control the risk.

My mother, on the other hand, is a risk seeker of sorts. She loves the thrill of risk-filled activities. In my not so wildest dreams, I could even envision her swimming with the sharks off the coast of Hawaii or running with the bulls in Pamplona. Needless to say, I had some interesting moments growing up watching them work out their differing opinions and approaches to risk.

Observing the extreme positions of the risk tolerance spectrum represented by my dad on one side and my mother on the other gave me a perspective of risk awareness that awakened my curiosity. What could cause such drastic differences between two people so dear to me?

What determines an individual's personality make-up? What makes one person the life of the party and another a shy wallflower? Some argue it's simply a matter of chemistry and genes while others point to environmental issues during a person's formative years. Most researchers agree it's a combination of the two.

To a certain degree, our genetic and chemical makeup is a strong influencer in determining our Risk Personality Type. I went through this in the section on the science of the brain earlier. I use the term influencer instead of determinant specifically because we do have a measure of control over our Risk Personality Type.

Since we've already looked at the chemistry angle let's examine the issue of a person's environment. Looking at an individual's parental upbringing, inherited behavioral traits, social status and life experiences, we can see indicators of personality formation. A person's chosen career path can speak volumes about their personality before they even open their mouth.

Like most people studying personality profiling, I carefully reviewed the findings of the Myers-Briggs Foundation from a risk tolerance perspective. Myers-Briggs outlines 16 distinct personality types and does a superb job at detailing the characteristics of each type. As a result, I devised my own scale of five distinct types of risk-taking personalities which correspond to different risk personalities as follows: 1) Risk-Avoider 2) Risk-Hesitant 3) Risk-Interested 4) Risk-Taker 5) Risk-Seeker. Each one is summarized below.

In general, most see risk in a negative light. They view risky behaviors as crazy or dangerous. At the other end of the spectrum, many view risk-taking as fun-filled and exciting. It gives them a sense of feeling truly alive.

Most of us, even the risk-averse tend to admire the risk-takers. They are the thrill-seekers and rule breakers we might secretly yearn to be. I'll start my list with those on the tamer side of the spectrum and progress to the daredevil variety. I'll alternate between male and female pronouns to show I'm an equal opportunity risk evaluator.

In the brain science section, I touched on certain personality traits and tendencies as they relate to risk. Combining this with the culmination of research on the topic led me to identify these five distinct personality types. The following section outlines them in detail, painting pictures from the perspective of where each sits across the spectrum of risk tolerance.

The Risk-Avoider

At the risk-averse end of the spectrum, we have the person who avoids risks at almost any cost. She tends to be an introvert and goes to great lengths to keep from embarrassing herself in public. The risk-avoider carefully considers her own circumstances before taking action and therefore is often found to be over-analyzing decision-making situations. Her overactive focus on the possibility of failure leads to missed opportunities since she shies away from taking chances even when the rewards seem attractive.

Quite often, the fear of failure paralyzes her with indecision. She stops at the brink and can go no farther.

One interesting facet of the risk-avoider personality is she tends to be a people-pleaser. This is logical since she does not want to risk displeasing someone thereby possibly alienating them. Risk-avoiders tend to be conforming, passive and pleasantly accommodating. They can become quite emotional when making risk-related decisions.

As one might surmise, risk-avoiders represent the safest lifestyle of all five risk personalities. They are less likely to get hurt, either emotionally or physically. They are more likely to be perceived as anti-social since they exercise a great deal of caution when it comes to forming friendships. On the romantic side, they are usually criticized for being commitment phobic.

Risk avoiders will never be seen as the life of the party. In fact they are probably the ones ignored as wallflowers. When in school, they rarely raise their hand when teacher asks a question. In group settings, they rarely volunteer for anything.

The Risk-Hesitant

Being a little more adventuresome than the risk-avoider, the risk-hesitant person is willing to take well-measured chances cautiously. He must always test the water before diving in. Taking a very methodical approach to risk assessment, the risk-hesitant guy gathers all the facts needed to make the best possible decision.

Essential to his approach is seeking out the advice of experts in whatever area is involved in the risk being contemplated. This can be somewhat of a double-edged sword since risk-hesitant people do not really trust the advice of others and want to do their own research. This dilemma can lead to the fear of making decisions about taking risks, though that fear factor is not as intense as that of the risk-avoider.

Like the risk-avoider, the risk-hesitant person tends to be left-brain oriented. He makes decisions based on hard facts and has the tendency to nitpick about minor details. Being influenced by facts and research, he tends to be unemotional when it comes time to make a decision.

The risk-hesitant has many of the traits of the risk avoider but to a lesser degree. He tests the water before jumping in. He shies away from situations of which he is unsure. He will take non-threatening risks but only when talked into it. Risk-hesitant people tend to have larger circles of friends than risk-avoiders. They tend to be followers, not leaders.

The Risk-Interested

In the middle of our five-point risk personality scale, we make the shift from introverted personas to extroverts. The risk-interested individual lives a more relaxed life, rolling with the punches. She takes life a day a time, handling stress without cracking.

She is more involved with her community than the two previous types and has strong social connections. Being more social in nature makes her more likely to be influenced by her peers to take risks. Seeing friends and acquaintances engage in risky behaviors captures her interest and that alone may prompt her to take the leap herself. As a willing participant, she finds herself going along with the crowd just for the camaraderie and does not get hung up worrying about the danger that might be involved.

Risk-interested folks represent the middle of the road. You're never sure which way they're going to go when facing any situation involving risk. The risk-interested are envious of people who do risky things and wish they could be in the shoes of those who do.

They want to get as much information and as much encouragement as they can get from those they trust before taking action. After they succeed in a risky situation they feel relieved and proud of their accomplishment.

The Risk-Taker

Getting to the fun part of the scale, we encounter the risk-taker. He is more independent than most and exudes self-confidence in the activities he undertakes. His stature as an individualist has him stepping out of his comfort zone regularly and trying things people around him might be too timid to attempt.

He is unafraid and willing to take chances when rewards appear to be within reach. The desire to be the center of attention pushes some risk-takers to push the safety envelope just to take center stage by showing off.

While the fear of public speaking traumatizes the majority of the population, the risk-taker is likely to grab the microphone and jump up on stage. Doing so gives him a thrill where others would cringe at the thought.

When in Las Vegas, he's the ringleader at the craps table being cheered on by the crowd betting on his side. His innate need to prove himself in front of his peers drives him to take ill-advised risks just for fun.

While usually not willing to go out of their way to look for adventuresome activities that involve risk, they're happy to go along with the crowd for such exploits without needing extra encouragement. They can be leaders but only if they are comfortably confident they can do what is needed. They get enjoyment from being the center of attention in-group settings although they don't press very hard to be in that position.

The Risk-Seeker

At the top of the scale sits the risk-seeker. Often prone to reckless abandon, she not only willingly accepts risks as they pop up but actively goes looking for them on a regular basis. She is quite impulsive and frequently puts herself in dangerous situations without regard for consequences.

She is competitive by nature with a burning drive to succeed and a sense of urgency that often causes her to act without thinking. She is not described as being well-grounded by her peers and seems to live for excitement. She dies of boredom when life becomes too predictable. She has a wide circle of friends but has little tolerance for laggards. She likes meeting exciting new people, even if she knows they may be unreliable or even dangerous to be around.

The risk seeker is the first to cast off inhibitions in a social setting. She may tend to be a heavy drinker at wild weekend parties and almost always drives way too fast. She makes an effort to be the center of attention in-group settings, especially at parties. The risk-seeker is personified by the statement "Live fast, die young and leave a good-looking corpse!"

Facing danger on a regular basis, risk-seekers are prone to injury. Broken bones go with the territory. They wear their bandages, slings and casts as badges of honor.

Proud of the fact they will try anything once, it's not unusual for them to be the first to volunteer for things even if they lack the experience needed. They figure they'll just learn as they go.

Snapshot Summary of Personalities

The Risk-Avoider
- Fears risk
- Analyzes circumstances
- Prone to indecision
- Misses opportunities
- People pleaser
- Wallflower
- Emotional

The Risk-Hesitant
- Cautious about taking chances
- Wants the facts
- Seeks advice
- Does research
- Less emotional
- Followers, not leaders

The Risk-Interested
- Mix of introvert and extrovert
- Middle of the road position
- Casual day-by-day view of life
- Goes with the crowd
- Proud of risks they do take

The Risk-Taker
- Fun-loving
- Self-confident
- Temptation for rewards overcomes fear of losing
- A showoff when taking risks
- Hesitant but willing center of attention
- Willing to push the envelope with a little encouragement

The Risk-Seeker
- Searches for new adventuresome thrills
- Approaches life with reckless abandon
- Burning drive to succeed
- Few inhibitions in social settings
- Enjoys being the life of the party
- Always the leader, seldom the follower
- Injury-prone

Finding the You

Did you see yourself in any of the personality types? Perhaps a combination of two? It is common to have different risk personalities in different situations, but you should be able to see an overall placement of where you fit. To help you get a further feel for your approach to risk, I have included in Appendix A, a list of questions that will help you think about your approach to risk. It is by no means conclusive and there will be many questions that don't apply to you, but your answers should reveal your overall tendency.

Regardless of where you fall on the spectrum, take heart in knowing that regardless of your personality type, you can learn to approach risk in a way that gives you the best chance of success.

Commercial Risk Personalities

Risk personalities can be determined for business entities as well. Generally speaking, the Commercial Risk Personality of a business is a composite of the individual Risk Personalities of the owners and executives of that business. In addition, there are the "rules of engagement" adopted by the organization by means of its charter, bylaws, standard operating procedures and such.

It would be advantageous for business owners to identify the risk personality of team members and potential team members as it will help improve communication among the stakeholders.

External Factors Can Change Our Risk Personality Type

Aside from our brain chemistry, and genetic makeup there are external factors and occurrences in our environments that can significantly alter our risk personality type.

A study done by Romeo Vitelli Ph.D. from York University in Toronto looked into whether or not we can change our personality. His study found the general consensus is that personality is shaped by early life experiences and tends to stay stable over time.

The personality traits we have as adults tend to grow out of the kind of temperament we had as infants and young children.

Having said that, Vitelli found personality changes can easily happen depending our experiences and other factors. As we take on different social roles such as major promotions at work these roles can affect our personality.

For that matter, simply growing older can mean significant personality changes. As we become more mature, we usually become more agreeable, conscientious, and develop greater emotional stability.

A study published in the Journal of Personality and Social Psychology by Nathan Hudson and R. Chris Fraley of the University of Illinois at Urbana drew some surprising conclusions. The study looked into the question of how many people wanted to change their personalities and revealed unanticipated results.

They found that many of the participants in the study made significant personality changes during the course of both 16-week studies. Those who did make personality changes expressed at the beginning of the study that there were aspects of their disposition they did not like and would like to change.

Researchers have found life changes such as these can bring about personality changes:

- Increases in available resources—more money, inheritance
- Decreases in available resources—foreclosure, business failure, bankruptcy
- Getting into a new romantic relationship, getting married or divorced
- Having or adopting children
- Getting older—more security-minded, less likely to take risks
- Realizing new opportunities such as a major new job offer or career change

The take away here is that if you find you fit within a risk personality group that is not consistent with your goals, there is hope for changing your approach. Perhaps, for instance, you are very risk adverse, but you want to pursue big pay-off opportunities. The more you understand risk, the more you will see that it is much like a game.

You can approach risk quantitatively and make educated predictions rather than blind shots in hopes of succeeding. There are times to take risks and there are times not to take risks, and we can never eliminate all aspects of risk. We can become seasoned risk takers who base our decisions to move forward with particular risks based on data and not exclusively hope or emotion.

Deep Dive Analytics

For the more analytical readers who want to look at a study with a more scientific approach than I have taken here, see Appendix C. There you will find the results of a risk profile study done by FinaMetrica, an Australian company specializing in risk profiling. In this study, the analysts at FinaMetrica divided the participants in the study into seven risk groups based on their risk tolerance levels. They provide a highly detailed characterization and statistical data on each of the seven groups.

In Conclusion

As individuals, we often think of ourselves in terms of how we would like to be in contrast to how we really are. Many old-guard conservative type people see themselves as risk-takers in their own minds. Knowing our risk personality type gives us a realistic view of our true approach to taking risks, allowing us to evaluate our risk-tolerance posture with respect to our goals and objectives.

YOU are your greatest resource. Take the time to understand your predispositions in an objective manner, as well as the intrinsic tendencies. The more you understand how you work, the more you can set yourself up for success.

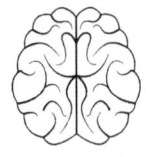

Chapter 5

RISK PROFILE

"Only those who will risk going too far can possibly find out how far it is possible to go."

—T.S. Eliot

The Anatomy of Risk

I have always had a fear of the ocean; I prefer to have marine wildlife in a nice controlled fish tank rather than feeling like I am in theirs. I have several friends who are scuba divers. Naturally, they want to share their love of the ocean with me and I decided that I didn't want to let a fear keep me from connecting with them in their passion. Being an avid "google-er," I looked to the internet to tell me about what I was risking by going scuba diving. I learned about the frequency of problems, which was lower than I was expecting. I also learned about risks that I had no idea even existed (forget sharks - the microscopic creatures are terrifying!).

I started snorkeling with a few friends. As we entered the water all of my fears surfaced as I wondered what horrors were lurking in the shadows waiting to "get me". As we moved through the water together, I saw a variety of sea life, including barracudas and stingrays. I don't know what I was expecting, but the experience was much less terrifying than I thought it would be, even with encountering these potentially dangerous sea creatures. The more I experienced the more I understood, and the safer I felt.

At the fundamental level, there are two types of risks; inherent risks and residual risks. I was inherently fearful of the ocean. However, after doing some research and listening to some basic safety protocols given to me by my friends, I felt a diminished (residual) fear of the ocean. So the goal is to change our inherent fears into residual fears by understanding them better.

How do we dissect risks to better understand their various aspects? If the fear of the unknown plays a large role in deterring us from taking a risk, understanding a risk can help us to make the decision of how to proceed much less subjectively.

The Risk Assessment

When you are examining risks that can potentially affect you or your organization, the first step is generally to conduct a risk assessment. A risk assessment is the overall process or method where you identify hazards and risk factors that have the potential to cause harm. You then analyze and evaluate the risks associated with those hazards. Finally you determine appropriate ways to eliminate the hazard, or control the risk when the hazard cannot be eliminated (risk control).

Risk assessments are an integral part of your safety plan. They bring awareness of hazards you or your organization are facing as well as identify who may be at risk. The assessment guides you through mitigating the risks you face as well as to create priorities in what you address.

Throughout the process you answer pertinent questions. What risks am I facing? What are the potential consequences of this risk? How likely is it to occur? Do I have the controls in place or should I add additional measures?

There are many types of risk assessments (financial, safety etc.). As a commercial risk manager, I have a process with resources I utilize to conduct risk assessments for my clients. Every process is different but I am going to present, conceptually, how a generic risk assessment is done. I recommend you bring in an expert who can help you provide the most thorough look possible of the risks you face.

Plan your Risk Assessment

Before you conduct your risk assessment you need to determine the scope of your evaluation. Be specific in what you are evaluating, such as "the financial risks of moving forward in an investment" or "the physical safety of your workplace", or "the hazards facing your organization". You will then gather the resources needed to perform the assessment. This may include human resources in the form of training a team to help with the process or involving stakeholders.

Informational resources should also be gathered such as any needed data. You then need to determine what type of analytical measures you will use to evaluate the risk. This would include the scale or parameters needed to provide the most relevant evaluation. There is a wealth of information online you can use to look up your particular risk that you are assessing.

Performing your Risk Assessment

There is no single way to perform a risk assessment. You have to determine the process or technique that makes the most sense for you or your organization.

For some a simple discussion can be the extent of risk assessment that is performed. For other risks a paid expert with an established team could be brought in to do an external risk assessment evaluation. Every situation is different. You can follow the rabbit hole of potential risks as far as you want to go.

At some point, it becomes counterproductive to continually evaluate risks to a degree that you are spending more time and money than is warranted. Assuming you are somewhere in the middle, I am going to run through the basics of a risk assessment. It is important to have a member of the team who is competent in risk assessments as well as someone who has a good understanding of the current operations.

Identifying Hazards

The first step in any risk assessment is to have a thorough look at your (or your business') environment to identify those things, situations, processes, etc. that have the potential to cause harm. Each risk is different and will have different criterial and questions for evaluating. If you were performing an assessment on handling dangerous materials in the workplace, for example, you would take into consideration the following:

- The location where the material is handled
- How long and how often the material is handled
- The methods and procedures used in handling the material
- The workforce training that has taken place to educate the employee on handling the material
- Common reactions should problems take place
- The equipment, tools, or safety devices used to handle the material
- The actual and potential harm of handling the material

Once you have identified your hazards you can rank and prioritize them from the most serious to the least serious, and which ones you think are most likely to occur to least likely to occur. This would be your impact or severity rating. This will help you determine what to spend the majority of your efforts on attempting to mitigate.

Impact/ Severity Rating

Impact rating is used to describe expected effects. The levels are as follows:
- **Very High**- The threat event could be expected to have multiple adverse catastrophic effects—financial, loss of irreplaceable objects, emotional stress, injury or death.

- **High**-The threat event could be expected to have severe or adverse near-catastrophic effects.

- **Moderate**-The threat event could be expected to have an adverse serious effect, probable not involving injuries and certainly not death.

- **Low-** The threat event could be expected to have a limited adverse effect.

- **Very Low-** The threat event could be expected to have a negligible adverse effect.

Once you have gathered this information, you can decide what measures or controls you should put in place to effectively eliminate or minimize the harm from happening. There are different ways you can respond to a risk.

Risk Response Type

Once you evaluate a risk, you then can determine the course of action you will choose. The options you have are as follows:

- **Accept-** Consequences of the identified risk, should they occur, will be accepted in the identified risk is within risk tolerance. No action will be taken.

  This option is taken if you decide to move forward without trying to control the risk in any way. Perhaps the costs of controlling the risk outweigh the potential impact. For example, you could decide that you are willing to accept the risk of a home break in and decide not to purchase a home security system.

- **Avoid-** Identified risk exceeds the risk tolerance. Specific actions will be taken to eliminate or revise the activities or technologies that are the basis for the risk.

This option is chosen when you want to move forward but you want to put safety measures in place to control the risk. For example, you could decide home ownership is too risky based on things such as a volatile housing market and decide to avoid it by staying in an apartment/hotel instead.

- **Mitigate**- A portion of the identified risk exceeds the risk tolerance and cannot be accepted. Actions will be taken to reduce the impact or probability of the risk to maintain risk at an acceptable level.

  You decide to manage the risk. You want to move forward but you aren't comfortable without some safeguards. You put a plan in place to protect yourself (security system, guard dog, etc.).

- **Share**- Share the responsibility and ownership of the risk to an outside resource or organization. You decide to move forward and maintain some level of risk but you also share a portion of it with another party.

- **Transfer**- Transfer the responsibility and external resource such as an insurance company.

Other Variables of Risk:

- **Probability** - The extent to which something is probable; the likelihood of something happening or being the case.

- **Vulnerability/weakness**- The quality or state of being exposed to the possibility of being attacked or harmed.

- **External factors** - Anything out of your control or anything that directly influences the outcome of the event. This would include compensating controls or mitigating factors.

- **Impact** - The effect of the event or cause; the end results after an event has occurred.

So, using a fear of sharks in my snorkeling experience at the beginning of this chapter as an elementary example, if I wanted to examine this risk I would look at it in the following way:

- **Probability** - According to the University of Florida's International Shark Attack file, my odds of being attacked by a shark would be just 1 in 11.5 million. I would be far more likely to be killed by a dog, snake, or car accident.

- **Vulnerability** - I don't possess the ability to defend myself should I be attacked by a shark.

- **External factors** - There are some areas that are more prone to shark attacks than others. Following professional recommendations as to where to swim will reduce the likelihood of a shark attack.

- **Impact** - Of 79 shark attacks that were reported worldwide in 2000, only 11 of them were fatal. Still, the impact of being bitten by a shark, emotionally, would certainly be traumatic to say the least.

Risk Formulas

Risk management professionals break it down into a scientific process that involves formulas, weighted questions, and calculations. They take it much further than is within the scope of this book. But there is one formula I want to present that, conceptually, will help you approach risks. This formula is primarily used in a commercial context, but it can be extrapolated down to the risks we take on a daily basis.

Determining the Risk Level

Risk level is determined by calculating the Impact value (I) multiplied by the Probability Value (P).

$I * P$ = Risk level (e.g. high, medium, low)

Impact - The effect expressed in financial terms
Probability- The likelihood of the impact happening

As a grossly simplified example on a personal level, say you are considering purchasing a home security system. Home security is an important concept to most people. The ability to feel safe greatly influences one's quality of life. When making the decision to purchase the system, you may look at the probability of a break in. The probability of the event happening depends on many factors, mainly geographic.

Data from the FBI 2012 crime report reveals that one in every thirty-six homes in the United States will be burglarized this year. The impact could be loss of valuables due to theft or injury or death to you or a loved one.

The exact value is not easy to determine - how can you put a number on the safety of yourself and your family? Strictly from a financial standpoint the average loss is $2,230 per break-in.

This would obviously be adjusted personally based on the invaluable keepsakes and other treasured belongings you keep in your home. The probability would also be affected by the safeguards you put into place to deter or defend against such an attack. Perhaps you have a guard dog or sleep with a gun.

You should take all of these aspects into consideration. For the sake of simplicity, the risk level could be determined by multiplying 1/36 - one out of every 36 houses are broken into - by $2,230 - the average amount of financial loss per break in. This number is $61.94. That may not be enough to justify the purchase of a home security system, considering most systems charge around $50 per month to monitor.

However, when looking at the safety element and peace of mind, making the calculation based purely on the calculated odds may not be enough to make you comfortable with a decision to go without a security system. Obviously, many elements of this formula will, often times, not be possible to quantify. The concept, however, is the key here: understanding the method for evaluating risks. The following table serves as a guide for determining the probability rating.

Probability Description

Rating

Near Certainty	90% likelihood that risk will occur
Highly Likely	70% likelihood that risk will occur
Likely	50% likelihood that risk will occur
Low Likelihood	30% likelihood that risk will occur
Not Likely	10% likelihood that risk will occur

Individuals and businesses face all kinds of risks, many of which can result in serious losses. The majority of large corporations have sizeable risk management departments whose job it is to monitor business operations and assets and limit the exposure to risk wherever feasible and practical. Private individuals and small businesses tend to deal with risk in a non-systematic way. Figure out a method that works for you and implement it in a way that makes sense for you and your organization.

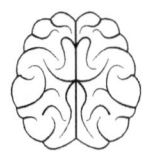

Chapter 6

SILENT RISKS

"The way to develop self-confidence is to do the thing you fear and get a record of successful experiences behind you. Destiny is not a matter of chance, it is a matter of choice; it is not a thing to be waited for, it is a thing to be achieved."

—William Jennings Bryan

Risk is certainly everywhere. What about the risks we involve ourselves in but don't take the time to consider the consequences of? Some risks are more obvious than others. This chapter covers risks we may or may not be aware that we are engaging in. I think of these as "silent risks." Ignorance can be bliss, but knowledge is power.

As you develop your skills as a risk manager, you can train yourself to be objective about the risks you are taking that you may want to reconsider.

I am describing a few here, some that are more obvious than others, but I encourage you to take some time to consider what "silent risks" you encounter on a daily basis.

Spending Decisions

It's been said that money is the root of all evil. I really can't bear witness to that but I can assure you that money is at the root of most risks. Who would associate going shopping with risky behavior?

Let's step back and look at the big picture. It's amazing how much more clarity we have when we're way up in the sky looking down! Unless you're Bill Gates or Richard Branson, there are finite limits on how much cash you have at your disposal for day-to-day purchases.

It helps if we think of personal spending as a zero-sum game. The more we spend on one purchase, the less we have to buy other things. What if splurging on that pair of shoes means we run out of money before our next paycheck comes? Not to worry. We have that marvelous invention of modern day society, the credit card. Just whip out that MasterCard, buy the darn shoes and get on with your day.

According to a 2016 Bloomberg report, the average U.S. household has about $16,000 in outstanding credit card debt and pays over $1,300 per year in interest. Putting the obligation to repay the $16,000 balance aside for a moment, that's $1,300 less we have to spend on other items—like daily necessities. Sean McQuay, NerdWallet's Credit and Banking Expert, says, "Taking on debt to cover the gap between income and expenses is a short-term fix with costly long-term results." That certainly sounds like a risky proposition to me.

Our big picture view makes it pretty clear that over-spending can easily lead to bankruptcy, or at least being forced to drastically lower our standard of living for a protracted period of time. We hear a lot about risk/reward but this is definitely a case of risk/punishment.

Health Risks

Pardon the pun, but taking risks with one's health is a sore subject. Cigarette smoking presents a dramatic paradox in the healthcare arena.

People know for certain it's extremely bad for their health yet they keep lighting up. Is it that they have a death wish or do they think they'll be incredibly lucky enough to beat the almost insurmountable odds they'll suffer from serious medical problems including death?

Tobacco use is the leading cause of preventable illness and death in the United States. It causes many different cancers as well as chronic lung diseases such as lung cancer, emphysema and bronchitis, heart disease, pregnancy-related problems, and many other serious health maladies.

Right behind the smoking habit comes our propensity for over-eating. Being overweight increases the risk of many health problems, including diabetes, heart disease, sleep apnea, osteoarthritis, liver disease, kidney disease and certain types of cancer. It's no secret that over two thirds of Americans are overweight and childhood obesity has become a national health crisis.

Also no secret is the fact that processed foods and fast foods are loaded with ingredients that represent serious health risks. So why is it that 75% of the population fails to do anything about it by changing their eating habits? Is it because we're too lazy or because the pleasure center of our brains overrule the cognizant awareness of the risk? Research studies indicate it's a combination of both.

Let's go a step further and look at a situation where findings have shown that preventative steps to ward off a disease may be more harmful than the disease itself…I'm referring of course to flu shots.

It wasn't too many years ago that getting a flu shot at the onset of flu season was seen as a prudent measure.

Now, medical journals have published thousands of articles revealing that injecting **vaccines can actually lead to serious health problems** including harmful immune system responses and a host of other infections. This can increase the body's susceptibility to the diseases that the vaccine was supposed to protect against. While the jury is still out on the flu shot controversy, getting these shots is now seen as a risk.

Cyber Risk—Personal

Accompanying the spectacular benefits the Internet has showered on us, the convenience of online information processing certainly has its dark side. It gave birth to a new breed of criminal activity, i.e. cyber-crimes. Millions of consumers have been victimized by cyber-thieves stealing personal information through Internet channels.

One of the most publicized incidents involving credit card information theft happened to Target Stores in 2013. In the middle of the Christmas shopping season, information in the company's point of sale computer system was stolen by highly skilled hackers who were never caught.

The names and account numbers of 40 million credit and debit card holders were downloaded from Target's computer system as well as personal data on 70 million customers.

While Target's CEO promised that consumers would not have to pay any fraudulent charges stemming from the breach, more than 90 lawsuits were filed against Target by customers and banks for negligence and compensatory damages. It was never determined how much financial damage consumers suffered but the breach cost Target over an estimated $188 million.

In addition to Target, many other retailers, commercial businesses and financial institutions had the personal information of its customers stolen by hackers operating on an international scale. Organizations affected include eBay, Home Depot, Sony Pictures Entertainment, Citibank, Heartland Payment Systems, Anthem, Ashley Madison, Tricare and JPMorgan Chase.

Identity Theft

While the piracy of one's credit card numbers signifies an immediate risk of financial loss, the damage criminals can do when they get their hands on your personal identity information can be far-reaching. A person's social security number is the golden goose of your identity most cyber criminals are after. However, they can do some significant damage with just your name, address and phone number in many cases.

Identity theft can happen to virtually anyone. According to a study done by the US Department of Justice (DOJ) in 2015, almost 18 million people in the US experience some form of identity theft each year.

Back in the old days, identity theft was most commonly done by a pickpocket boosting your wallet or a thug accosting you in a dark alley. Now it's done with a few keystrokes on a computer terminal, PC or even a smart phone by a cyber hacker.

The most common harm identity theft victims suffer is financial loss, which can be either direct or indirect. Money stolen from you by an identity thief is immediate and visible. Indirect losses, such as legal fees and reputation damage, can continue to mount in the aftermath of the theft and may plague you for months.

The average loss per theft incident was about $1,350 according to the DOJ's 2014 study and the total losses attributed to identity theft for the year exceeded $15 billion.

Usually more damaging than having a hacker obtain your credit card numbers is when they use your identity information to open new accounts for their own use. Most credit card companies have become pretty skilled at detecting the bulk of fraudulent situations, but there are still a large number of illegitimate transactions that slip past their safety net. Many of these can hang around for years.

A victim's credit score can be weakened or even decimated by fraudulent account activity perpetrated by the criminal. Delinquent credit card balances and defaulted cash loans are the most prevalent problems that destroy credit ratings. In many cases, victims may only be made aware of the damage when they have a credit card application or loan request denied.

Credit score problems caused by fraudulently opened accounts take the longest time to get resolved by the credit reporting agencies.

Identity theft doesn't just impact victims financially, it also often takes a significant emotional toll. A survey from the Identity Theft Research Center found that 69 percent felt fear for their personal financial security, and 65 percent felt rage or anger. And, almost 40 percent reported some sleep disruption. These feelings increased over time when victims were unable to settle the issue on their own, according to the report. This can result in problems at work or school, and add stress to relationships with friends and family.

Ramsomware

Having its origin in Russia, ransomware is a type of malicious software that has spread rapidly throughout international computer networks in the past few years. It is electronic extortion in which a hacker sends out legitimate looking files in hope that unsuspecting computer users will download them.

Once downloaded into a PC or computer network, the malware blocks the user from accessing their data until a ransom is paid. Payments are demanded in bitcoin digital currency for which traceability is virtually impossible. Supposedly when the cyber thief receives the ransom money, he or she will send the user a code to 'unlock' the computer.

As would be expected, many users never receive this code.

Simple ransomware locks the system in a way which a knowledgeable PC user can remedy without paying the ransom. More advanced malware can encrypt the victim's main directory table and entire hard drive, rendering the computer totally useless.

Cyber criminals are now using advanced cryptography to encrypt stolen files making it harder and harder to detect and disarm. These diabolical hackers are getting increasingly adept at disguising their devastating links and downloads as harmless.

The hacker might pose as one of your service providers saying you need to fill out a form to keep your service or warranty current. They may also employ social media hacking to pose as someone on your contact list to get you to click on a link in an email.

Reputational Risk

One characteristic we all have is our reputation. It relates directly to our self-worth. Most people care dearly about their reputation, going to great lengths to protect it. In the minority there are those who could care less about their reputation. Hardened criminals represent the extreme case of this but there are many who take a nonchalant view of their reputation.

A tarnished reputation can manifest itself in a number of ways:
- Being convicted of a blue collar crime
- Being fired from a job for moral turpitude or incompetence
- Being addicted to drugs or alcohol or being known as a heavy user of these substances
- Becoming known as a trouble-maker
- Getting into serious financial trouble such as a foreclosure or bankruptcy

Gambling Risk

While everyone knows that gambling involves risk, many of us engage in it anyway. It ranges from a poker night with friends to a weekend trip to Las Vegas or Atlantic City.

In a friendly neighborhood game the odds are even for everyone at the table. When you set foot in a casino, there is no such thing as even odds.

The house always has the advantage. And the house's advantage varies based on your game of choice. It's normally based on the size of the potential jackpot. The larger the chance of winning the big one, the lower the odds are of winning it.

Your first tip of just how powerful the house's advantage is should be obvious just by seeing the terrific ambiance of some of the Las Vegas casinos. The opulent structures were not built by winners!

Steve Wynn, the most prominent casino owner has a net worth of $2.4 billion as estimated by Forbes. This was not a matter of luck. It was carefully calculated. He once boasted on a television interview that the house keeps a whopping 20% of every dollar bet in his casinos. Yet people pour in by the thousands to try their luck.

Job Risks

It's common knowledge that some jobs are riskier than others. The most common of jobs considered risky are typically those that endanger one's health and even the chance of death.

According to Bankrate.com, here's the list of the nine riskiest jobs:

- **Logging workers** - Dangers involve operating heavy machinery and working in bad weather and at high altitudes. In the sawmills, it's common to see workers with missing fingers.

- **Commercial Fishermen** - Malfunctioning gear, nasty weather in turbulent seas and traumatic boating incidents cause many injuries and fatalities. This profession has the 2nd highest fatality rate in the US.

- **Roofers** - Falls are the leading cause of fatal injuries, but even lesser injuries such as broken bones cause construction work to be ranked as one of the most injury-ridden jobs.

- **Garbage Collectors** - One would normally not consider this an overly dangerous occupation, but statistics indicate abnormally high injury and fatality rates. Like heavy machinery, garbage trucks are dangerous to be around.

- **Farmers and ranchers** - Working around heavy machinery is once again the culprit. Transportation equipment ranks as the highest cause of serious injuries. Farming also carries a heavy financial risk. A bad crop year can do serious damage to a farmer's bank account.

- **Structural iron and steel workers** -Installing heavy iron or steel beams with cranes is no walk in the park. Falls, slips and loss of balance give ironworkers one of the highest rates of injuries.

- **Truck drivers** - Long hours on the road make this a very tough job. High expectations of the transport companies lead to overworked and exhausted drivers. Traffic accidents are the major cause of fatalities.

- **Electrical power line workers**—Working high up in the air with electrically charged equipment spells potentially fatal conditions on a daily basis. Electrocution and falls are the biggest dangers.

- **Aircraft pilots and flight engineers**—Airplane crashes and emergency landings are the obvious danger of these jobs.

Needless to say we all face risks on a daily and sometimes hourly basis. One can hardly leave the house without facing risks of some nature. Wait a minute—there are even risky situations that occur in the house. It seems we're not safe anywhere.

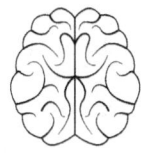

Chapter 7

TOTAL COST OF RISK

"If you are not willing to risk the unusual, you will have to settle for the ordinary."

—Jim Rohn

Being an insurance professional, I deal with buyers at varied levels of sophistication. One of the primary differentiators between the two is an understanding of the *Total Cost of Risk*.

I was speaking to a potential client recently who had seen rising insurance premiums in their manufacturing business and wanted to shop the market to see if they could get a better price. This individual paid hundreds of thousands of dollars every year on their insurance, and wanted to minimize these costs however they could. "I want the cheapest policy you can find" the customer told me. I told them that my approach was more of a risk manager and that I wanted to help them control their total cost of risk, not just the cost of their policies.

I attempted to explain how there are many aspects that go into the total cost of risk, beyond just what they pay in insurance premiums. After reviewing their policies and procedures, I saw a major gap in some safety controls that likely could prevent many of the accidents that were undoubtedly raising their premium. I suggested a customized safety program that would help get these costs under control.

Ultimately, the buyer went with a competitor that offered a policy 5% lower than what I presented. What they failed to realize, is that the policy they bought had a deductible much larger than the policy I presented. There were also exclusions that were likely to occur in their environment. Most importantly, they had no plans to proactively prevent the accidents that were affecting their insurance, loss of productivity, reputation, etc.

Sophisticated buyers recognize that insurance premiums are only one cost of their risk management budget. There are many aspects that go into controlling the total cost of risk, and these are applicable to both commercial and personal policies.

What is Total Cost of Risk?

There are many costs associated with the risks we take. First, there are the insurance premium costs for those risks we decide to cover. Then there are retained losses such as deductibles, uninsured losses and exclusions. There are also additional costs we incur to protect ourselves, both internally and externally.

On the personal side for example, we may pay for a home security system. Even though we pay homeowners insurance, this is another cost we incur to provide protection.

My favorite analogy illustrating these costs is in the form of an iceberg. When you look at an iceberg, you only see a little bit poking out on top of the ocean. Below the surface of the water is a MUCH larger mass of ice. The ice on top represents the direct costs you pay for insurance. The bottom of the iceberg represents all the indirect and uninsured costs.

These hidden costs include time to investigate, time to hire replacements, onboarding costs, training costs, productivity loss, downtime, tool/equipment damage, product/material damage, legal fees, extra supervision etc.

When we take risks based on our decisions, we need to develop the ability to look at the whole picture. As is the case when we decide to purchase insurance, it is the most visible cost we pay to control risk that is necessary to keep us protected.

When I looked at my health insurance quotes this year, my eyes were quickly drawn to the lowest monthly premium. But then I looked down to the "total out of pocket" number, which was a game changer for me.

It does me no good to pay $300 monthly for a policy with a high deductible if I expect to have health care costs that exceed the deductible. This pretty much guarantees my total out of pocket cost would be higher than if I were to pay for a more expensive policy that had lower deductibles and probably better coverage.

The bottom line is this: there isn't one "right" or "wrong" way to manage risks. Each person, each business, and each circumstance has unique criteria that should be examined individually. The additional deductible and the extra costs one would incur for incidents that are not covered need to be calculated as part of the total cost of risk.

Controlling Commercial Total Cost of Risk

What we have seen so far is that risk is everywhere. And like almost everything else in business, risk comes with a price tag. In order to control it, we must measure it, and measuring it is the beginning of the process to keep the cost associated with risk to a practical minimum. That is the responsibility of an organization's risk management unit.

The cost of risk is a quantitative number. The total cost of your specific company's risk is broken down into its component parts: insurance premiums and deductibles, retained losses, and the cost of controlling risk, both internal and external to the organization.

By itemizing and examining these component costs, we can implement strategies to minimize them as much as is practical. We can't and don't want to eliminate all these costs or minimize them to the bare minimum because some expenditures are necessary to protect our assets and profitability.

Cost of Insurance and Deductibles

These costs are the easiest to quantify, monitor and control. You know the costs of your policies and what all is protected with each one. You need to regularly review what is and is not covered as business conditions change.

If you don't have an experienced broker who provides policy auditing as a value added service, there are professional auditors who will come in and thoroughly examine your policies and find things on which you may be have a gap in coverage or have duplicate coverage. These adjustments will probably lead to either a cost increase or cost reduction.

Being insured for items you don't need insurance on is the main cost savings these specialized auditors will identify. Your policies can be adjusted, lowering the premium. But that in itself is not a free service. An auditor's fee is normally a relatively small percentage of the savings realized. This fee of course is part of your total cost of risk.

The deductibles you pay when losses are incurred are also a known cost and need to be added in. Attorney fees expended to defend against lawsuits fall into this category as well.

The Cost of Safety Measures

I've already discussed the cost of liability insurance. But the true cost of protecting your employees and customers from injury goes beyond insurance premiums. Examples of these are the costs of safety equipment, the cost of preparing safety documents and procedures, quality control costs associated with making sure your products meet safety regulations, employee training, warning signs, safety barriers and such.

The Cost of Business Losses

All business expenses and lost sales due to risks that hurt you financially need to be tallied as part of the cost of risk. For items that are insured, the cost may be limited to the amount of the deductible. But what about the more intangible costs such as sales opportunities lost due to a risk gone wrong?

These costs will probably be only an estimate but they are important to the bottom line; so they need to be quantified. The sales dollar volume lost of course is not the true loss. The expected gross margin is the true loss and that can be estimated with a reasonable degree of accuracy.

What's the cost of damage to an organization? To a large degree, that's a number that defies quantification. Like lost sales, however it can be estimated. Let's say your sales dropped off 10% for six months after a well-publicized product recall or legal incident where the company was found to be guilty of fraud. Again, the gross profit margin of the sales drop is added in to the total cost of risk.

Productivity Losses

When employees are injured on the job, insurance coverage and possible OSHA fines are not the only costs involved. Paid employee time off recovering from injuries and a below average productivity level as they fully recuperate diminish their job productivity.

Drops in productively levels have a negative effect on profits. Also coming under the category of lost productivity is employee time spent investigating incidents and cleaning up after spills and damage.

Insurance Overview

Insurance is a necessary business expense to manage risk. Not all policies are created equal, and there are no substitutes for a good agent or broker who can help you navigate the process. I am now going to do a basic briefing on the different portions of an insurance policy. If you need help with terminology, Appendix B includes a glossary of insurance terms. Becoming familiar will help you be a more informed buyer and help you make sure you are buying what you need.

An insurance policy is a legally binding contract between the insured person or business and the insurance company. The insured is also called the policy holder. The policy states in detail the financial amounts the insurance company is obligated to pay the insured in various type of incidents. The amount the policyholder pays is called a premium.

Many insurance policies are written according to standard forms provided by ISO (Insurance Services Office.) They include a great deal of boilerplate text which many policyholders fail to read or fully comprehend. This is the reason for most of the disputes between policy holders and insurance companies.

Again, a good agent or broker can help policy holders understand the really important aspects and nuances of each policy.

Insurance policies are typically integrated contracts. This means they include everything that spells out the agreement between both parties. In some situations additional documents, especially formal letters sent by either party add items to the policy which render it a non-integrated contract.

Legally, every stipulation in the policy at the time of original signing as well as documents written later as riders or endorsements are binding as long as both parties give their consent. Oral agreements are governed by the parol evidence rule which means they will not be accepted by a court if the policy "appears to be whole." In addition, advertising materials are typically not included in a policy and thus, are not enforceable.

The Insurance Policy

An insurance policy has separate parts. Understanding the different sections will help you find the information you need and know what to look for when you are reviewing your policies.

Declarations — Here you will see the official name of the insured along with the address, the insurance company providing the policy, the policy limits for specific perils, i.e. the maximum to be paid and all associate deductible amounts.

I want to take some time to explain deductibles, as it is often a misunderstood concept. A single policy may contain several different deductibles. For example, the wind/hail deductible may be $25,000 and the "all other perils" deductible may be $1,000. It is important to know how the deductible is applied: per occurrence, per location, per item, or per claim.

With a single deductible amount you can have several deductibles in one event.

Also be aware that some deductibles are percentages (in contrast to flat deductibles). The percentage deductible can apply to the claim, or it can apply to the building value, the building and building personal property value on the policy, or it can also include loss of business income.

Many policies include a retention, and many people think this is the same as a deductible. Although it is similar, it is treated totally different. With a deductible, the carrier will pay the claim, deducting the amount of the deductible before payment.

With a retention, the INSURED must actually pay the retention amount before the carrier will pay for anything. And that can include defense of the claim. I know this is getting into the weeds a bit, but understanding this element of your coverage is crucial to understanding the policy.

Insurance agreement—This describes the covered perils and details of the coverage policy. This section describes the promises made by the insurance company, i.e. the promise to provide indemnification to the insured.

Policy form—The insurance contract along with all conditions, declarations, exclusions and definitions are usually combined into one integrated document. When a policy needs to be customized beyond what is provided in the declarations portion of the standard policy, the underwriter may attach appropriate riders and/or endorsements.

Terms & Conditions—Obligations and any other duties to which the insured is required to comply in order for the policy to remain in effect and for claims to be paid.

Exclusions—These provide specifics about what is not covered under the policy that might otherwise be assumed to be covered. It is worth mentioning that exclusions often provide some of the very best coverage.

Endorsements—Addendums attached to the policy to expand upon, revise or delete clauses included in the standard insurance form(s).

Riders—Similar to endorsements, riders are used to amend, further define and/or extend standard policies. They are attached to the original policy the same way as endorsements.

Jacket—This term may be used differently from insurer to insurer. It typically refers to a preprinted brochure which contains all policy language except that contained in the declarations page and endorsements of a specific policy. In the jacket are found the insuring agreement(s), standard exclusions, conditions and definitions.

Definitions—Several pages included in a policy to clearly define all terms in bold print used in the policy. The definitions are provided to eliminate confusion or misunderstanding between the insurance company and the insured parties.

BEWARE of these 5 Insurance pitfalls

This is by no means meant to be a definitive list on what you need to be aware of when it comes to insurance pitfalls, but I am including five to be on the lookout for.

Exclusions. Often, there are sneaky little exclusions put into insurance contracts that void important coverages. The other day I spoke to a trench digging company who was very proud about their low insurance rates. When I looked at their policy, I realized they had a "subsidence exclusion" which excludes claims involving earth movement. I would say a trench digger needs to have coverage for earth movement. Without it, you could be in for an ugly surprise when damage occurs.

Also know, you can add coverages and change limits. Adding coverage can be done by adding an endorsement to the policy. When you are selecting your coverage and limits, go back to your risk assessment. What are your risks? Which of these risks do you want to retain and which do you want to transfer to your insurance company? If this loss did happen, what would it cost you to be made whole again?

Co-insurance. A co-insurance penalty is one in which the insurance company pays only a stated portion of the financial amount of a claim after the insured party has paid the deductible. For example, if you only purchase $250,000 of homeowners insurance and your house is worth $500,000, you will not have secured 80% minimum of coverage.

So, if something happens, the insurance looks at it as if you decided to "self-insure" for 50% of the value, so the insurance company may only pay 50% of the claim.

Deductibles. A deductible is the stated amount of money the insured party must pay in an insurance claim before the insurer must pick up the remainder of the full claim up to the policy limits and conditions in the wording of the policy. Be careful that you are aware of what your deductible is and be prepared to pay it should you have a claim. If you are more concerned with getting the premium lowered and you are prepared to cover a higher deductible, you can sometimes have your premium cost lowered as you agree to raise your deductible.

Actual Cash Value (ACV). Be aware that in a property claim, the ACV for which you are compensated may easily be less than what it will cost you to replace the piece(s) of property at current market prices. Essentially, it devalues your property for wear and tear during the time you owned the property. The way to avoid this shortfall in compensatory damages is to purchase full replacement value insurance.

Beware of ignorance. So many people assume they are covered when they are actually not. Take the time to look into what insurance you have and what insurance you need, both personally and professionally. You may decide to not choose a particular coverage, but let it be an informed decision and not a decision by neglect.

Chapter 8

COMMERCIAL RISK

"You've got to take risks if you're going to succeed. I would much rather ask forgiveness than permission."

—Richard Branson

An Overview of Business Insurance Categories

As you may recall from the Anatomy of Risk chapter, there are different ways we respond to risks: we can accept them, avoid them, mitigate them, share them, or transfer them. This chapter is devoted to the last of these responses, to transfer risks. We typically transfer them by securing insurance. Because commercial insurance is so complicated and not as straight forward as personal insurance, I'll keep the focus of this chapter on commercial risk. If you are not mitigating commercial risks, feel free to skip over this chapter.

Business insurance is multi-facetted. Without boring you with a few hundred pages of all the gory details, I'll summarize the basics. Keep in mind these are general descriptions to give readers a bird's eye view of the subject. Business owners should consult an expert on business insurance coverage before making key decisions on what kinds of insurance are appropriate for keeping both your risks and premium expenses as low as possible.

There are several "players" in the game you need to be aware of:

The Carrier

Carriers are insurance providers (Hartford, Travelers, Chubb, etc.). There are lots of options out there, and they all have different elements to their policies. For example, a policy purchased through Travelers may be very different from a policy from Hartford. There is a rating system that focuses on the insurance industry. Both the U.S. Securities and Exchange Commission and the National Association of Insurance Commissioners have recognized this rating system as the industry standard. It is called the A.M. Best and measures insurance companies' financial strengths or weaknesses.

Its ratings are as follows:

"Secure" Ratings:
- **A++, A+** (Superior)
- **A, A–** (Excellent)
- **B++, B+** (Good)

"Vulnerable" Ratings:
- **B, B–** (Fair)
- **C++, C+** (Marginal)
- **C, C–** (Weak)
- **D** (Poor)
- **E** (Under Regulatory Supervision)
- **F** (In Liquidation)
- **S** (Rating Suspended)

Companies that A.M. Best follows but does not issue a Best's Credit Rating on are designated as Not Rated (NR). Insurance carriers either work through insurance brokers or are "direct writers" meaning their own agents are exclusive to them and work directly with consumers.

There are advantages to both. Brokers represent you to multiple insurance carriers, and we will go more into how they work in the following section. It is also advisable to see if the carrier or broker offers additional services that may save you money in other areas. For example, if they perform safety audits you could have access to loss control services. For these services, you'd paying extra for if you sought them independently.

Direct writers can sometimes, but not always, have less expensive policies because they cut out the middleman. Remember that direct writers work for the insurance company, not for you. On the flip side, brokers represent multiple companies, allowing them to shop for the policy that suits your needs for the best price.

The Broker/ Agent

Insurance brokers serve as go-betweens between insurance buyers and insurance companies. They are similar to direct insurance agents but represent the buyer rather than the insurance company.

Brokers vary in expertise, personal drive and initiative. They also vary in what insurance markets they represent. The way they represent a market is by receiving appointments from the insurance carriers. If a broker sells a policy from a particular carrier for example, the broker needs to be contracted with that carrier.

Brokers vary in expertise; you want an agent who knows and understands policy and coverage language. Another differentiator is the range of services they provide, which can vary from broker to broker. Some services to look for are the following:

- Loss control services
- Risk management services
- Claims management services
- Ancillary services (human resource support, analytics etc.)

I have seen good insurance brokers and not so good insurance brokers. My recommendation is to find the right insurance broker who will proactively work with you to control your total cost of risk and not just sell or renew your policy annually. There are strategies as to when you go to market. Naturally, different carriers provide quotes that differ in coverage and premium cost. To get a selection of quotes from which to choose, you need someone who is thinking strategically instead of just checking to-do items off a list.

A good broker should be working with you to find you the best possible package. They effectively represent you in dealing with different carriers to achieve this. You're best to find a broker who is passionate about going above and beyond the services of an average agent as they're shopping policies for you.

I recommend that you interview several brokers and compare them with quality and services offered in mind. Take the time up front to select one you are sure has your best interests at heart and is equipped to provide you with the services you need. Once you do, it is not advisable to shop different brokers year after year unless your broker of choice falls short on working closely with you on a long-term strategy.

Brokers are marketing your account to different insurance carriers. If you use multiple brokers to obtain quotes for you, keep in mind they are often checking with the same carriers; it becomes a race to be the first to submit to a particular carrier. The best brokers refuse to work with clients who take this approach and the insurance carriers are less likely to take you seriously if they keep seeing submissions under your name year after year.

A good strategy may include "going to market" once every three years or so. You should definitely meet with your broker 3-6 months before renewal to discuss market trends and the best approach for the current year.

The Underwriter

The underwriters are responsible for evaluating your risk and determining the premium. They work for the insurance carrier. They are important because they decide if you are a good risk or a bad risk and have the authority to offer certain credits or debits to your premium. The goal of a good insurance broker is to make their client "best in class" among other businesses with similar risks.

Businesses in the best class get the best rates. Brokers can also get feedback from the underwriter of a carrier and ask: "What can we do to make this business a more attractive risk?"

I spoke to an underwriter on behalf of a client recently who said "You know, I am really uncomfortable with this certain aspect of what your client does." Knowing their concern, I was able to explain more about the safety protocols in place. And we added a few based on their recommendations. The client, who was facing non-renewal, was renewed without a rate increase based on us getting recommendations from the underwriter and putting them into practice.

Types of Business Insurance

Employee Health Insurance

After the costs of wages and salaries, employee healthcare expenses are the next largest employee-related spending item for most businesses.

Health insurance is changing rapidly, and influenced heavily by legislation and policy changes. The future is widely unknown and highly speculative regarding what the healthcare landscape will look like in the future. I would, however, like to include this expense in the total cost of risk. The cheapest policy is not always the greatest, and the indirect costs of not offering good options should be taken into consideration.

For the sake of an overview, the following terms and concepts are important to know when selecting and purchasing health insurance. The language of health insurance can be hard to understand. Yet, it's becoming increasingly important for the people in a company who are responsible for health care insurance administration. It's also good for insured employees to have a good understanding of the industry's terminology. Keep in mind this is a partial list covering only the most important items.

- **Claim**—a request by a plan member, or a plan member's health care provider, for the insurance company to pay for medical services.

- **COBRA**—An extension of a member's company group insurance coverage after terminating employment. Premium costs will be paid by the employee only.

- **Coinsurance**—the amount you pay to share the cost of covered services after your deductible has been paid. The coinsurance rate is usually a percentage. For example, if the insurance company pays 80% of the claim, you pay 20%.

- **Copayment**—one of the ways you share in your medical costs. You pay a flat fee for certain medical expenses (e.g., $10 for every visit to the doctor), while your insurance company pays the rest.

- **Deductible**—the amount of money you must pay each year to cover eligible medical expenses before your insurance policy starts paying.

- **Exclusion or limitation**—any specific situation, condition, or treatment that a health insurance plan does not cover.

- **Group health insurance**—a coverage plan offered by an employer or other organization that covers all the individuals in that group and their dependents under a single policy.

- **Health maintenance organization (HMO)** - A health care financing and delivery system that provides comprehensive health care services for enrollees in a particular geographic area. HMOs require the use of specific, in-network plan providers.

- **Health savings account (HSA)**—a personal savings account that allows participants to pay for medical expenses with pre-tax dollars.

- **In-network provider**—a health care professional, hospital, or pharmacy that is part of a health plan's network of preferred providers. You will generally pay less for services received from in-network providers because they have negotiated a discount for their services in exchange for the insurance company sending more patients their way.

- **Network**—the group of doctors, hospitals, and other health care providers that insurance companies contract with to provide services at discounted rates. You will generally pay less for services received from providers in your network.

- **Out-of-network provider**—a health care professional, hospital, or pharmacy that is not part of a health plan's network of preferred providers. You will generally pay more for services received from out-of-network providers.

- **Out-of-pocket maximum**—the most money you will pay during a year for coverage.

- **Pre-existing condition**—a health problem that has been diagnosed, or for which you have been treated, before buying a health insurance plan.

- **Preferred provider organization (PPO)**—a health insurance plan that offers greater freedom of choice than HMO (health maintenance organization) plans. Members of PPOs can get care from both in-network or out-of-network providers, but member costs will be lower for in-network providers.

- **Waiting period**—the period of time that an employer makes a new employee wait before he or she becomes eligible for coverage under the company's health plan.

Property Insurance

Covered Property

Property insurance protects business owners against losses related to the real estate, structures and building contents within their place(s) of business. It also typically can cover damage or destruction of property belonging to other parties that are on the insured's premises.

The insured location can be owned, leased or rented and be covered under the policy.

While some policies are standard forms, many policies are drafted by insurers themselves. Almost all of them are based on the general Insurance Services Offices (ISO) property policy and thus are adapted to the standard form issued by ISO itself. I will explain how typical policies are assembled.

Building coverage normally includes machines and equipment that are permanently installed, such as a furnace, a boiler, and air conditioning equipment. Anything else permanently attached to the building(s) is also covered. This could be items such as: permanently attached manufacturing equipment, or mechanical equipment, or even an over-head crane, used for lifting.

Business Personal Property (BPP) consists of property you own that does not qualify as building property and may include items such as office furniture, machines and equipment (if not attached to the building), raw materials, goods-in-process and finished goods. Improvements and betterments you make to a leased building are covered if you paid for them and they cannot be legally removed.

Two types of property you don't own may also be covered: 1) Items you lease that you are obligated under a contract to insure; and 2) property in your care that is located inside the building or adjacent to the building. But watch your limits! Make sure you have increased the limits for each to match the exposure.

Excluded Property

The following types of property are excluded under virtually all property policies:
- Money and securities, accounts
- Animals other than stock used in production
- Vehicles, aircraft or watercraft
- Land, docks and wharves
- Crops located outside
- The cost of excavation or land moving

Additional Coverages

Almost all property policies also include sub limits for certain other costs such as: electronic data, debris removal, fire department charges and increased cost of construction.

Most commercial property policies cover all damages or perils not specifically excluded. The "causes of loss" section lists the types of damages that are excluded. Excluded items typically exclude damage caused by things such as flooding, earthquakes and trickery.

Casualty Insurance

Casualty insurance covers loss or damage to the business itself. It typically covers commercial liability, but some may include personal coverage as well.

There are several different types of casualty policies, each one you have to buy separately:

- General liability insurance, including general liability
- Workers compensation and employers liability coverages
- Commercial auto insurance
- Commercial umbrella coverage
- Specialty coverages such as special event insurance
- Errors and omissions (generally for professional services)
- Employment practice liability coverage (EPL)
- Cyber coverage
- Directors and Officers coverage (D&O)

Crime insurance protects a business against loss or damage to property or certain goods due to criminal activity. These typically include such things as robberies where money or securities were stolen, employee theft, vandalism and such. Equipment breakdown coverage protects against loss or damage caused by a major failure of machinery or equipment.

Some casualty policies cover items not classified as third-party liability. An example is commercial auto physical damage insurance. This coverage is actually a type of property insurance. It protects a business against physical damage to vehicles owned by the business that do not fall under a typical motor vehicle policy.

Workers compensation insurance is actually a form of casualty insurance even though it isn't liability coverage per se. It pays benefits to workers injured on the job on a no-fault basis. Injured workers need not file a lawsuit against their employer to obtain benefits. Worker's comp policies do not cover third-party liability. See the Workers Compensation below for more information.

Liability Insurance

Liability insurance covers incidents of liability legally imposed on your business due to negligence of the business itself or its employees. When your business is being sued for actions that are illegal or can be represented as negligent, this is where liability coverage comes into play.

Active Shooter Coverage

An active shooting incident is defined as one or more individuals actively engaged in killing or attempting to kill people in a populated area. And, incidents are on the rise. 70 percent of incidents took place in either a business or educational environment, and the largest percentage took place in a business.

Following active shooter incidents there are frequently lawsuits claiming negligence on the owner of the establishment where the incident took place. The Department of Homeland Security (DHS) provides a variety of no-cost resources to enhance preparedness and response to an active shooter incident.

There is a huge misconception about being covered in these situations. Because of the ambiguity in the language of the insurance coverages, in the wake of an incident the company could face a nasty battle with the insurance carrier.

There are a different coverages out there, and they vary in what is covered. When you are selecting one, you want to find one that covers risk assessment and crisis management services, as well as event responders and post-event counseling services. You may want to find one that also includes an onsite active shooter vulnerability assessment, as well as preparedness training. Part of the vulnerability to negligence lawsuits is lack of preparedness.

Employee benefits liability insurance

This type of policy covers claims that result from errors in administering employee fringe benefits. It protects companies from employee lawsuits stemming from administrative errors. Even small clerical errors can have major consequences.

Employee benefits errors are not covered by commercial general liability policies since, most of the time, they don't result in bodily injury or property damage. They can cause only financial damage, which is not covered by typical liability policies.

Examples of administrative liabilities covered:
- Describing benefit plans and eligibility rules incorrectly to employees and family members.
- Failure to maintain accurate employee benefits records.
- Failure to include an employee's beneficiary in a life insurance plan.

The need for employee benefits liability insurance coverage depends on factors such as the number of employees on the payroll and the types of benefits available to them. It gives the company protection against major claims filed by employees and/or their dependents.

Companies that employ a small workforce or one that does not offer many employee benefits may not be able to justify the cost of this insurance.

Liability for Loss or Damage to Electronic Data

Most general liability policies contain many electronic data exclusions such as the loss or damage to data stored on computers or the inability to access such data.

General liability policies regard electronic data as intangible property and thus is not defined as property damage covered by these policies. A separate policy, rider or endorsement is typically required for this coverage.

Bodily Injury and Property Damage Liability

Who and What is Covered?
Acquired companies and or newly created subsidiaries

A typical liability policy automatically provides coverage for most new business units for one month regardless of whether the insurer is notified. It works like personal automobile insurance for newly acquired vehicles.

Many policies exclude joint ventures and LLCs. The insured company must own 51% or more of the new business unit in order for the policy to go into effect automatically.

Additional Insureds

Insured companies may include other entities or persons on their policies as long as both parties sign a written contract agreeing to the coverage. Below are examples of typical additional insured parties.

- Distributors — Individuals or other companies who sell your products or services
- Equipment Lessors — Owners of machinery or equipment you have leased
- Property managers and landlords — Independent parties who manage your properties
- Independent Contractors — sub-contractors or general contractors hired by you

Exclusion: Damage or injuries that are expected or intentional

Liability policies do not cover damages or injuries that are either anticipated or intentional on the part of the insured. However, injuries sustained through the use of "reasonable force" for personal or property safety reasons are covered.

Exclusion: Failure to disclose hazards

When and if an insurer determines that the insured party has lied or concealed material information about the risks it faces in the conduct of its business, claims can be denied and policies canceled. Such acts prevent the insurer from assessing the risks it is insuring against.

Surety Bonds

Not fitting into either the property or casualty insurance categories are surety bonds. They do still qualify as insurance in that they protect against a loss but they are not truly considered insurance policies. A surety bond is a legally binding contract that ensures obligations to an obligee by a obligee. The principle is the person or company providing goods or services to the obligee.

To protect the obligee against non-performance on the part of the principle, the principle may be required to purchase the surety bond. When and if the principle fails to deliver according to the contract, the surety company will compensate the obligee financially.

Management Liability Insurance

Insurance that covers exposure faced by directors, officers and managers of a business. Such exposure may arise from governance, finance or management activities that are deemed to harm other parties.

Directors' and officers' liability policies are typically purchased by large corporations to protect the principles for errors or omissions (E&O) they commit while performing their duties on behalf of the corporation.

E&O insurance does not cover situations of bodily injury or property damage and only compensates injured parties for financial losses. It is typically required by companies or individuals that provide professional services as their primary business.

Employment practices liability insurance protects companies in cases where employees are suing the company for acts such as harassment, discrimination and wrongful termination.

Medical Payments Insurance

These policies cover medical expenses for people injured on company property or job sites being managed by the company. Injured parties do not have to prove the company itself is liable for their injuries, only that the injuries occurred at company facilities. Injured parties might be customers, vendors, visitors or even simply passersby. The coverage typically has a very low sublimit- perhaps $5,000 or $10,000.

Commercial Auto Insurance

Although your personal automobile policy may imply on the surface that your vehicle is covered at all times, this is usually not the case if the vehicle is used for business. This is the case even if you're a sole proprietor using your car for business such as making sales calls.

Drivers who use their cars part time or full time working for car services such as Uber or Lyft are usually not covered by their personal policies while on the job. If your business owns vehicles required to be titled by your state, you need a commercial auto policy. Commercial auto coverage insures against property damage and personal injuries caused while you're driving the company-owned vehicle.

Many business owners fail to carry adequate auto liability insurance. If several people are injured in an automobile accident caused by you or one of your employees while on company business, your company can be sued for bodily injuries that may reach into the millions of dollars. Sole proprietorships or small companies can easily be destroyed by such judgments.

When purchasing commercial auto coverage, many business owners focus on the vehicles they own but forget to cover those owned by someone else, like a rental car or vehicle owned by an employee who is using it for business purposes.

Mobile equipment like forklifts, graders, tractors and bulldozers need to be covered by a commercial auto policy if it's not covered by the general liability policy. Such mobile equipment must be licensed for road use and must be added to the auto policy for liability.

When mobile equipment is being operated at a job site or on your premises, it is covered for liability under your general liability policy.

Certain types of ancillary equipment and even automobiles are covered automatically under most commercial auto policies. Examples are small trailers (under 2,000 pound capacity), towed equipment or vehicles used as temporarily substitutes for out-of-service vehicles.

If you or someone in your company is involved in an auto accident and the matter goes to court, typical commercial auto policies will cover legal costs incurred.

Workers Compensation Insurance

If you have employees, you are required to have coverage for them concerning on-the-job injuries. Every state has different regulations and guidelines for workplace injuries, but most have some form of workers' compensation system.

The states closely monitor and enforce rules stating that payments for medical bills and damages are made quickly to employees suffering injury. Some states allow an employer to opt-out of the system if the employer is self-insured. Concerning independent contractors, rules also vary from state to state. To free themselves from the liability, many states mandate that the employer proactively ensure that each contractor is adequately covered for job-related injuries at his or her own expense.

While workers' compensation laws cover most workers, there are some not included and these exceptions can vary between states. In most states, independent contractors, sub-contractors and domestic and agricultural employees are not covered. Some states even exclude real estate agents.

Workers' compensation laws call for payment of benefits regardless of who is at fault. Benefits must be paid to employees who sustain injuries due to their own negligence or that of a co-worker.

Workers Comp Benefits

Benefits to killed or injured employees are set by state laws, which are fairly consistent from state to state.

- Compensation for disability is a partial amount of an employee's lost pay during the period of disability. If the disability is permanent, the benefits could go on indefinitely.

- Compensation for rehabilitation also include vocational training expenses for employees no longer able to function in their former job because of their injuries.

- Reimbursement for medical expenses cover physician fees, tests, hospital stays, nursing care, prescriptions, and any physical therapy required by a doctor.

- In the cases of death, benefits are paid to the surviving family members including minor children.

Determination of employer premiums

Workers' compensation premiums are calculated based on two main criteria, remuneration and relative workplace dangers. The workplace dangers are determined by the employer's benefits payments compared to the average payments made by other employers in the same industry and geographic region. Larger total benefits payments are assumed to be tied to worker safety.

Business Interruption Insurance

In situations where a business is unable to sustain its operation due to a direct physical loss, such as a fire that wipes out a good deal of it facilities, business interruption insurance is available to cover loss of business income during the period of restoration.

Such damages are mostly in the form of loss or substantial

degradation of its normal income and cash flow.

Definition of Business Income

The covered income of a business generally includes the net income the business is projected to earn if the interruption had not happened. Also covered are fixed operating costs such as lease payments, rent, utilities and property taxes.

These policies are also available to businesses owners who rent or lease facilities to other businesses or individual residents. In cases where structures become uninhabitable due to perils such as fire or extensive water damage, the insured can be compensated for lost rental income. Business interruption policies typically don't cover relocation or temporary facilities for the tenants, but extra expense policies do. Many loss of income forms include extra expense.

Restoration Period

The loss of income a company sustains due to a business interruption is based primarily on the length of time required to fully repair damages. There may be a waiting period before compensation benefits kick in. If a business relocation is required, the restoration period and benefits end when the company is able to resume business at the new location.

Life and Disability Insurance

Many companies carry life and disability insurance for executives and other key employees essential to the business. This is most common in businesses structured as partnerships because the business is likely to face hardships due to the loss of a partner.

In such policies, partners normally name the partnership as the beneficiary. With the funds received from the settlement, the remaining partners often use the funds to buy the deceased partner's interest in the business from that person's estate. This is often called "key man" life insurance.

Commercial Umbrella Insurance

This type of policy covers damages beyond the limits of other liability policies held. This type of policy increases the limits of any liability provided by other policies, known as underlying policies. Usual underlying policies include general liability, auto liability, and employer's liability.

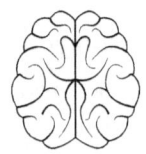

Chapter 9

STAYING POWER

"What you have to do and the way you have to do it is incredibly simple. Whether you are willing to do it is another matter."

—Peter Drucker

Naturally, we couldn't conduct a survey on risk without addressing one of the biggest challenges to our success: the temptation or tendency to quit when the going gets tough.

When we take on big or complicated risks we are almost guaranteed to encounter roadblocks. If you quit every time you are challenged then you are guaranteed failure. Life is full of challenges! We must develop the internal fortitude to know when to quit and when to keep fighting. Just like risk itself, this decision is one that can be approached without passion or prejudice. Take a healthy step back and look at the situation objectively.

Steps to Keep You in the Game

Focus on your vision. Make sure your vision is written down. It's a little trick of the mind, but things that are written down are more likely to stick in your mind. Post it in a place you're going to see it at least once a day and read it daily. Make sure everyone working with you sees your vision statement frequently.

If you can paraphrase your vision into a short tagline, put it on your business card and on the business cards of anyone else in the company who carries them. Most importantly, when you lose sight of what your dream is or why you are doing, what you are doing go back and look at your vision. As the scripture goes, "without vision the people perish".

Positive "What If" Musing. Envision the positive "what ifs." What if my new product is a home run? What if I exceed my sales targets? What if a new hire turns out to be a super star? What if I land a few new big customers I thought were long shots? What if my business takes off and expanding becomes a necessity?

Focusing on the positive keeps you positive, and what you focus on grows. If you are one of those analyzers who like to think of every little thing that can go wrong I would like to challenge you to stop the pattern of negative thinking. Once you have itemized the significant things that may go wrong, make a plan of action on how to attempt to avoid these consequences. Then put them out of your mind and get back to the positive.

Get Some Sleep. Sleep is vital to our health and well-being. Our bodies require long periods of sleep in order to restore and rejuvenate, to grow muscle, repair tissue, and synthesize hormones. We feel more alert, more energetic, happier, and better able to function following a good night of sleep. It also plays a critical role in thinking and learning.

Lack of sleep can make you grumpy and foggy. Studies show that sleep loss and poor-quality sleep lead to accidents and injuries on the job. Lack of sleep hurts our cognitive processes by impairing attention, alertness, concentration, reasoning, and problem solving. This makes it more difficult to learn efficiently. Plus, when a person is tired they are generally negative, and we must stay positive to be successful.

Quit Stressing Out. Stress drains your precious energy that should be put into getting things done properly and in a timely manner. Medical researchers agree that stress itself is a health hazard that can easily lead to illness, often serious illness. Excessive stress increases the risk of obesity, heart disease, Alzheimer's disease, diabetes, depression, gastrointestinal problems, and asthma.

> "Stress increases the risk of obesity, heart disease, diabetes and other ailments."

Let's face it, there are problems that pop up in our businesses and in our personal lives over which we have no control. They just happen. Stressing over them does absolutely no good. It will not make them go away; so why ruin your health and productivity worrying about them?

Ignore Naysayers. Stop listening to people who habitually tell you why one of your ideas is bad or even impossible. But don't mistake naysayers for people who take a genuine interest in your success. These are the ones who give you wise counsel and even play the devil's advocate when they spot danger signs in an area you're pursuing. Surround yourself with positive encouraging people who you can trust to give you sound advice.

Stay Committed. Once you have decided to take a calculated risk, put your chips all in and be totally committed to seeing it through. Being half-hearted about a goal almost guarantees failure. Be sure those around you are right there with you and committed to success. There is, however, one possible downside to this. If thing go terribly wrong and it becomes obvious that your idea or project is doomed, have the wisdom to abandon it before you drive your company over the cliff.

Mind Your Health. Because new ventures are exciting, they can turn you into a workaholic before you know it. You spend so much time chasing success that you start ignoring important matters in your personal life. One of the most important aspects that suffers first is your health.

Beyond stressing over things that go wrong as we mentioned above, you may also find yourself skipping meals or possibly worse, dashing through the drive-in window at a fast food restaurant. These rob you of the nutrition you need to function at your optimum level. Be sure you take time to eat healthy meals and don't be in such a rush that you miss doctor's appointments.

Make Time For Family. Without healthy relationships with your family and friends, your interests will narrow, making your life less fulfilling. Spending quality time with family and friends will not only relieve stress but will make you a more well-rounded person. This will also result in your being a more pleasant person in the workplace. Workaholic bosses can easily become hardened to peoples' feelings, since they don't take time to relax with people they love.

A family who feels the husband and father is never around becomes unhappy and even bitter and rebellious. This can be the same or even worse for workaholic mothers. When conditions at home reach the crisis point, the workaholic parent must abandon some of their responsibilities at work to fix the situation at home.

If a workable balance is not struck between work and family, divorce may be the result, which leads to even bigger problems.

Smell the Roses. Hardworking entrepreneurs must take time off from the workplace grind to do things totally unrelated to their business venture. Simple things like going for a walk, listening to relaxing music, doing some meditation or just sitting by a lake or river and thinking about life can be a refreshing break.

You will return from such activities rejuvenated with a sense of calmness and happiness which can work wonders in your place of business.

See the Big Picture. Don't let the small problems cause you to lose focus of the big picture. With all the risks a business owner must take on a daily basis, things can get chaotic. Staying focused on the big picture will steady you and enable you to stay the course and not feel like your workday is a wild roller coaster ride.

Remember if you appear to be in a chaotic state, your employees will be distracted from doing their jobs properly. It can be a nasty ripple effect.

Abandon Investment as the Last Resort

Unfortunately, despite our best efforts, some risks just don't pan out. I recommend, in your planning phases, knowing what criteria you have for knowing when to consider calling it quits. That way you don't give up on a whim, but you also don't keep throwing good money after bad.

Quitting, or giving up is seen as shameful in many cultures. It's perceived to be a sign of weakness or lack of tenacity or both. This stigma can unwittingly keep us on a path into the abyss and can make our recovery much more difficult than it has to be. Not only is it feasible to give up with dignity, but it can save us from financial disaster. There are times when listening to our instincts just makes sense for our sanity.

Coming to the realization that a payoff is less than what was hoped for is not the end of the world. You should make sure, in the long run, that you are compensated for the effort you are putting forth. Realizing this is not the case does not equate to giving up in the negative sense. It is merely a realistic appraisal of the bleakness that will face us if we stubbornly fail to see the inevitable.

Business Staying Power

If business was easy, almost everyone would own their own business. The shocking reality of just how hard it is to succeed with your own start-up hits almost as soon as the ink is dry on your business license. The Small Business Administration (SBA) states that 22% of new businesses fail during their first year and almost 50% fail within 5 years. Many others estimate those numbers are worse than SB statistics.

These numbers tell the tale that the odds are stacked against the average start-up. How do you as a budding entrepreneur get the odds in your favor and end up being among the 50% that are still in business after the 5 year mark?

Make sure you have a well-crafted strategy, a solid business plan, adequate start-up capital and a proper business location. These elements are probably the most critical keys to success. Even with those things in place however, the road to success is still strewn with potholes that must be skillfully navigated. The most vital element in making that happen is staying power—the resilience and persistence to keep going during the tough times that are certain to happen.

When one encounters rough patches such as losing a major customer or a new product release that does not go as expected, thoughts of throwing in the towel may start running rampant. This is most prevalent with the risk-hesitant and risk-avoiders.

It's inevitable that many risks big and small don't pay off. The entrepreneur who suffers a setback on the road to success must toughen up and keep moving forward. Too many start-up owners succumb to the urge to give up prematurely before they achieve success. It's staying power that keeps the persistent ones driving forward in spite of risks going awry.

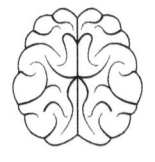

Chapter 10

FAMOUS RISK TAKERS

*"If things seem under control,
you are just not going fast enough."*

—Mario Andretti

You'll recall I pointed out earlier that almost all of us tend to admire people who seem to be natural-born risk takers, even if their personalities are not considered likeable or their causes do not seem honorable. Many people assume daredevil personas vicariously when watching action-packed movies or extreme sports events, many times without even realizing they are doing so.

Just for fun, let's take a close look at a few of the more notable, and even notorious people we have read about in the news or seen on television.

Bill Gates - Microsoft

After his first few years at Harvard, an entrepreneurial Bill Gates took a risk that would put him on a track to become the richest man in the world. He dropped out of college to launch a fledgling start-up in his garage that would end up becoming Microsoft. Abandoning his parents' desire for him to become a lawyer, Gates decided to jump headfirst into the business sector dominated by industry giant IBM.

Unafraid of being swallowed up by IBM, he partnered with the behemoth and delivered the first operating system for the IBM PC. He accepted $50,000 from IBM but ran the risk of retaining the copyright to the software instead of going for a much larger payoff. The risk paid off handsomely as his PC-DOS operating systems became the industry standard, dwarfing the value of the $50K stipend.

John DeLorean - General Motors and DMC

After designing a series of highly successful cars including Pontiac's GTO, Firebird and Grand Prix, John DeLorean became the youngest division head in the history of General Motors. In an attempt to parlay his success into a personal fortune, he voluntarily left General Motors to start his own company, DeLorean Motor Company (DMC), in 1973. He turned the heads of the big automakers and the driving public with his new DMC-12 with its all stainless steel body and gull-wing doors.

Unfortunately, it took 8 years to get the DMC-12 off the assembly line, only to be met with a depressed auto market and a series of lackluster reviews. DeLorean's company was in financial distress. Desperate for money to save his company, DeLorean was somehow drawn into a large cocaine trafficking deal that would bring him

$24 million but was busted in a highly publicized sting operation by Federal agents. He was eventually found not guilty, but by then DMC was in bankruptcy and DeLorean's reputation was toast.

Elon Musk - PayPal, Tesla Motors, SpaceX, etc.

After launching, building and selling PayPal for many millions, everyone expected Elon Musk to follow that brilliant start with another Internet-based tour de force. He instead showed his 'wanderlust' for exploring all corners of the business world. His stated vision was to change the world and even humanity itself.

A next step in his quest was taking a stab at reducing global warming through sustainable energy. He co-founded Solar City to mark that off his bucket list.

Taking the gains from PayPal, Solar City and a few other ventures, he took a huge risk by investing in two innovative startups, Tesla Motors (luxury electric vehicles) and SpaceX (space exploration). Trying to operate these two highly diverse ventures simultaneously nearly spelled financial disaster for both. Overcoming many ominous obstacles, Musk and his investors now reap the rewards of two thriving and well-respected corporations.

Musk will now most likely begin to focus on perhaps the riskiest venture yet with his plan to reduce the "risk of human extinction" by "making life multi-planetary" with the establishment of a human colony on Mars.

J.K. Rowling - Author

Who would ever think that being an author could be considered a risky profession? It's hard to believe that publishing Harry Potter was ever considered to be a "risk." J.K. Rowling's struggle to find someone who believed in the book enough to publish it was a long, tough journey.

She was a single mother living on welfare, so spending all her available time trying to get her book published was taking valuable time away from her efforts to put food on the table.

Even in the face of one rejection letter after another, she refused to stop believing in her book. This is a sterling example of having staying power in spite of a big risk that I mentioned earlier. Rather than giving up, she took the risk of hiring an agent to help get the book to the market.

One bleak and worrisome year later, she finally got the call from her agent. Harry Potter and the Philosopher's Stone was to be published by Bloomsbury Publishing in London. Her many loyal readers are grateful for her taking that risk and sticking with it.

Sylvester Stallone

What's so risky about being an actor? Well, the path Stallone chose to work his way up to Hollywood stardom was riskier than most people realize. With a baby on the way and too little money to pay the rent on his apartment in tinsel town, Sylvester Stallone sat down and wrote the screenplay for *Rocky*. Producers loved it and offered him big bucks for the story but would not let him play the lead role.

Although he was struggling financially and on the verge of being homeless, Stallone refused to sell the *Rocky* story if the producers would not allow him to play the lead role in the film. They finally gave in and let him have the role even though the money they would pay him as an actor was considerably less than what they would have paid him for the screenplay itself.

As we now know, his stubborn risk was well worth the eventual reward. *Rocky* ended up earning millions of dollars and Sly's rise to fame has become a Hollywood legend.

Michael Eisner — Disney

Being touted as the savior of the Disney corporate empire due to his revitalization of the beleaguered entertainment giant in the late 1980s and the dramatic success of Disney Tokyo, the emboldened CEO Michael Eisner set his sights on the European market.

With high hopes for a Euro-Disney chart-topper, Eisner crafted the development of a new Disney theme park near Paris, which opened in 1992 amidst significant controversy.

In retrospect, Eisner totally misjudged the risk factors involved in this massive project. He was even pelted with Brie cheese when he made the announcement in front of the Paris Stock Exchange. In spite of the fact that he was able to negotiate a fabulous land deal for the site, he failed to grasp the nuances of the French culture. Accusations of Eisner foisting "American cultural imperialism" on France dampened enthusiasm and attendance was dismal. Disney tried enforcing an appearance code like they do in the United States, but French labor unions saw that as an "attack on the workers' individual liberties."

On top of Eisner's erroneous judgment calls, an untimely recession and a collapse of the French property market sent the project's finances into a tailspin — one from which Eisner never truly recovered.

Buzz Aldrin, Neil Armstrong, Michael Collins - Astronauts

If you think jumping off a cliff strapped into a hang-glider apparatus is a risky proposition, imagine buckling into the command module atop a space rocket loaded with highly volatile explosives underneath you.

In the mid-1960s, John F. Kennedy took a bold risk in announcing that the U.S. would put an American on the moon before the end of the decade. That risk paled in comparison to the risk Buzz Aldrin and his fellow astronauts Neil Armstrong and Michael Collins took when they rocketed off toward the moon not knowing if they'd ever return.

To escape the earth's atmosphere, the Apollo 11 spacecraft had to reach a velocity of more than 25,000 miles per hour…and that's just the start of the journey.

Personally, I can't imagine jumping out of an airplane with a parachute even though a million people have done it safely before me. Think of the uneasy feeling Buzz Aldrin and Neil Armstrong had in the pit of their stomachs when jumping out of Apollo 11 onto the surface of the moon, almost a quarter million miles away from home!

The Wright Brothers - Aeronautics

Just sixty years before anyone even dreamed of flying into outer space, almost no one could conceive of humans taking flight like a bird and coming back to earth safely. Orville and Wilbur Wright were the first people to fly a plane that was heavier than air. They flew kites and gliders to gain experience and test data…not much risk in that.

Then came the day in Kitty Hawk, North Carolina in 1908 when it was time for the ultimate test and of course the risk of death or serious injury if a crash landing would mark the end of their brave experiment. The first flight lasted just 12 seconds and the plane flew only 120 feet, but the risk paid off and the aeronautics industry was born.

We can see from these real-life stories that not all big risks have to involve life-threatening situations. One thing is fairly certain though; fame and fortune do not come to those unwilling to take significant risks.

Chapter 11

THE LAWS OF RISK-TAKING

"Do not be too timid and squeamish about your actions. All life is an experiment. The more experiments you make the better."
—**Ralph Waldo Emerson**

From all the research I've done on the subject of risk, I've summarized what I have learned in what I call the "Eleven Laws of Risk Taking".

Law #1 — The biggest risk you can take is not taking a risk

For those who may be the less tolerant Risk Personality type, this first one is for you. At some point, you have to take the leap. As Mark Zuckerberg, the founder of Facebook said, *"The biggest risk is not taking any risk... In a world that's changing really quickly, the only strategy that is guaranteed to fail is not taking risks."*

Since you are reading this book, I can infer that you want to be successful and that you are willing to challenge yourself to be so. For the most part, other than for adrenaline purposes, as humans we are inherently opposed to risks. We are not, however, opposed to success. Big rewards often come from big risks.

Here's a little more on Elon Musk, who I mentioned earlier. After raking in millions on PayPal and a few other successful ventures, Musk took one of the biggest risks of his career causing many to question his common sense. He invested his last $35 million in cash to start Tesla Motors and mass produce the first luxury electric car line. The bold move paid off when Tesla's net worth topped $2.5 billion.

Let's move from high tech to the grocery store market. In the late 1970s, the demand for locally grown, organic, healthy food was virtually nonexistent. John Mackey and Renee Lawson Hardy decided to take a risk by leaving their popular grocery store chain. They took a huge step into what they saw as an untapped market with high potential.

A venture that could have died on the vine turned into Whole Foods Market, the now highly successful natural food store chain, which was just purchased for 13.7 billion by Amazon. I would say their risk turned out.

Law #2 — Avoid Paralysis by Analysis

Paralysis by analysis is certainly not a new concept. What is relatively new is that it's gotten worse. The amount of information with which to do research on any given subject has increased dramatically over the past 5 years or so due to increased use of the Internet—Google, Yahoo and Wikipedia specifically.

Instead of making decisions easier, this deluge of information leads to longer hours of reading facts and opinions adding to the confusion in decision making. A LexisNexis survey showed that the average employee spends more than half their workdays receiving and managing information rather than using it to do their jobs.

This confusion can lead to high anxiety, indecision, and dissatisfaction according to a study done by psychologist Barry Schwartz at Swarthmore College in which he called this phenomenon the "Paradox of Choice." The resulting dilemma leads to increased fear of making a wrong decision, which makes any decision appear more risky.

Summarizing a 2015 article in Work Lifestyle by Becky Kane we find the aspects of overthinking a decision as:

Overthinking lowers your performance. Especially on mentally-demanding tasks, overthinking taxes our short term memory to the point of not being able to store and analyze the proper information needed to get the job at hand done.

Overthinking kills creativity. A Stanford research study found that overtaxing our brain with information impedes our creative thinking. A recent Stanford study suggests that over-thinking not only impedes our ability to perform cognitive tasks, but also keeps us from reaching our creative potential as well.

Another Stanford study confirmed that absorbing and processing too much information stresses the right brain, leaving the creative left-brain to fall short of functioning the way it should.

Overthinking leads to unhappiness. Way back in 1956, economist Herman Simon created the term "satisficer" to describe the decision-making style that 'prioritizes an adequate solution over an optimal solution.' This concept essentially says that striving for perfection, i.e. the perfect solution, creates a problem of its own. While a person toils away crafting the perfect product, someone else introduces a similar product that is adequate to get the job done and captures the market.

Don't overanalyze to the point that you don't take the risk. There will always be reasons not to take risks, and the timing will never be absolutely perfect. You have to decide to move forward with gusto and determination.

Law #3 — Improve your Risk IQ

The scary part about risk is the unknown. You will never be able to eliminate all of the unknown from a risk, but you can become a better risk analyzer. You can remove some of the blind emotion and improve your risk management skills.

Hopefully you took the Risk IQ pre-test at the beginning of this book. As a conclusion, it is repeated again for a post-test. If you don't have a perfect score keep working at it until you do. Review material and find trusted professionals who can help you implement some of the strategies. Having a perfect Risk IQ doesn't mean you are immune to bad risks, but it does mean you are better prepared to be a risk taker than someone who is not familiar with these concepts.

Law #4 - Be open to counsel

Feeling proud of your knowledge and the achievements you've accomplished is natural when you've reached the level of executive or being considered a professional in your chosen career field. In spite of the expertise you've gained thus far in your career, you must come to grips with the fact that you don't know everything. Those who don't are in for a rude awakening. No one expects you to know everything.

So, how do you fill that gap? It's as simple as knowing where to go to get the extra spurt of knowledge and advice you need to get to the next plateau.

Even for those who are still building their careers, realize that getting help is just plain smart.

Sometimes our friends and loved ones are the first to realize we're going down a path that won't lead to success. Swallow your pride and take heed in what they're saying.

Learn to recognize the wisdom you can pick up from those around you, especially peers and co-workers. As we progress through life, there are things to which we are blind from time to time. The sooner you remove those blind spots, the faster success will become a reality.

If you have difficulty accepting constructive criticism, you're missing out on a spectacular opportunity to better your life and advance your career. Be aware, however, that sometimes what is passed off as constructive criticism is just the negative tirades of a naysayer or personal jabs from someone threatened that you may outperform them.

Don't expect quality constructive feedback to be given without asking for it directly. Many people will shy away from offering it for fear of hurting your feelings or losing a friend. Once you ask for the opinion of others concerning your performance, they may not only offer you valuable advice for improvement but will gain respect for you just for asking. Remember, it's not only your boss who can help you succeed.

Most businesses have formal programs in place to give you feedback in the form of annual performance reviews. In too many cases, these are more administrative in nature than constructive. Most bosses are too busy to put in the real effort to give you the genuine guidance you need in a performance review. If you make a personal request for their feedback in a pleasant, non-defensive way you will likely get the advice you need.

Many companies have formal mentorship programs but the

majority do not. Don't use it as an excuse if your company does not assign you a mentor, go out and find one yourself. Perhaps it's a college professor or a talented employee in your company who will gladly become your informal mentor. This can be your most valuable career management tool; use it as often as you can without being a burden to your mentor.

It can be a great way to build advocates that will open up new opportunities in the future. If you cannot find one in your own company, you might try some creative business networking to find one in another firm.

In addition to using a mentor for advice, you can also use them as a sounding board for your ideas. A good mentor will objectively listen to all ideas, even those that might sound a bit crazy at first. Remember, when you're brainstorming, there's no such thing as a bad idea. A wise mentor can help you sort them out and refine them.

Law #5 — Ignore bad advice

Just as it's important to be open to receiving constructive criticism, being constantly at the mercy of the "peanut gallery" will surely put you back into a state of paralysis by analysis. It's easy to say "ignore bad advice," but how do you tell the difference between good advice, useless advice and bad advice?

Sometimes your experience, common sense and reasoning are adequate to tell the difference. Other times, you need to do some due diligence on the person giving you advice to determine if they're qualified on the subject at hand.

Here are a few signals not to trust advice you're getting from someone:

- You strongly suspect or it's even obvious the person has a hidden agenda. Be alert to the person who has a hidden agenda.

- It's apparent the person giving the advice has an axe to grind.

- The person is simply repeating trite advice that's outdated or potentially harmful.

- The person's advice appears to be aimed at pitting you against someone else for personal gain.

In addition to doing your due diligence with the help of third party sources, there are some pointed questions you can ask the advice giver directly: How did you arrive at that conclusion? Do you have any background information that proves what you're saying is true? Do you know if anyone else has been successful doing what you're suggesting?

It's mind-boggling to me the number of people I meet in the business world who are handing out bad advice regarding fake solutions to nonexistent problems. Asking some penetrating questions to get at the root of the problem will often uncover more accurate information.

Never take advice at face value when someone's telling you not to try something if the advice is from a person who tried it and failed. Do your due diligence before dismissing it because in many cases, they were the problem. There will always be nay-sayers putting down your ideas or people trying to convince you of something for their own personal gain.

Law #6 - Embrace the "stupid" phase

There will be a phase when you start something new where you will not fully know what you are doing. Forget ego and just embrace it.

Remember the words of Richard Branson, "If somebody offers you an amazing opportunity but you are not sure you can do it, say yes — then learn how to do it later!"

I'm sure we've all heard the sage advice, "The only stupid question is one that is not asked." Don't be afraid of asking questions that others will claim to be stupid. One out of ten ideas may turn out to be brilliant. Learn to brush off the other nine as risks worth taking.

Just as you should not be ashamed of asking stupid questions, you should not be derailed when you make a mistake.

When you ask a stupid question or make a mistake, be proud of the fact that you actually did something of action rather than sitting on the sidelines. Mistakes and thoughtful responses to stupid questions make great learning opportunities; pay attention.

Make it apparent you're using it as a lesson learned. People have patience and respect for humble people and disdain for haughty know-it-alls. The situation you want to avoid is one where you pretended to know something and then be found out later. Now that's cause for embarrassment and the lesson learned is not to do it again.

Law #7 - Learn from others mistakes

If one thing is certain in life, it's that we all make mistakes. Learning from your own mistakes enables you to progress and failure to do so sentences you to years of repeated failure. That's a given, but there's a follow-on technique that's less painful and assuredly more effective. Learning from the mistakes of others puts you ahead of the game.

As we progress through life on both the personal side and in business, we gain knowledge from experiences of our own and those of people around us. When we make a mistake ourselves, we are painfully aware of it. If someone else makes a mistake and it directly affects us, we're sure to remember it and hopefully learn from it.

However, there's a third situation that often escapes notice. If someone else makes a mistake that has no effect on us personally, do we take notice? If not, we're missing a golden opportunity for a free lesson to learn from someone else's error.

It does mean we have to pay attention to what is going on around us. That's not as easy as it sounds since most of us tend to focus only on things that directly affect us. It does take some effort to notice and analyze situations outside of our immediate surroundings.

Getting beyond notorious things we read in the daily news, the real valuable insights can be found in books, especially self-help manuals, leadership books and autobiographies. Many successful entrepreneurs are not afraid to admit their mistakes in print—many even relish it. They take pride in the fact that they overcame some pretty serious mistakes on their road to success and enjoy telling the story.

Take, for instance, the story of Abraham Lincoln. During the 25 years before being elected President of the United States, he suffered through at least 10 major defeats, many through errors in judgment. Many of those were defeats in elections for a number of political posts. He learned from those mistakes and kept moving forward until he finally reached the pinnacle of success, President of the United States.

But let's get back to the business world for us mortal men and women toiling in our careers. In addition to learning from books, there is a wealth of lessons to be learned from others and part of this involves lessons they learned from their miscues. This of course can come only from mentors and advisors who are honest and forthright with their charges.

Law # 8 Know your Exit Point Criteria

I recommend having "Exit Point Criteria" that you establish when going into a risk - when you are still dazzled by rainbows and blue skies. The exit point criteria delineates when to call it quits if things don't go as planned. This keeps you from staying too long and from leaving too early.

Once you have made the decision to go for it, don't let anyone give you cause to doubt it. Use your exit point criteria. Remember this criteria may need to be reevaluated along the way. Don't let others talk you out of quitting when you get scared or discouraged. Surround yourself with positive people who empower you in your quest.

Law #9 - Recognizing a "sunk cost"

One rather tricky and sometimes misleading factor in assessing risk is the issue of sunk costs. Sunk costs are differentiated from anticipated and planned cost in that they are funds already spent and irretrievable.

Thus, when calculating risk/reward factors, only the anticipated and planned costs plus future operating cost need be calculated. One must come to grips with the fact that what is gone is gone for good unless some of the equipment can be salvaged, used elsewhere or liquated at a decent price. If so, this amount should be deducted from the actual cost when doing the calculation.

If the remaining funds required to complete the project plus operating cost will yield a profit, odds are good you're better off completing the project and

> "If the completed project will not yield a positive ROI, it's probably best to cut your losses."

absorb the budget overrun. If the completed project will not yield a positive ROI, it's probably best to cut your losses and abandon the project.

Sometimes we take a risk that looks great, but we discover other information along the way, something changes, or for whatever reason it just doesn't pan out. In the business world, sunk costs are usually involved. You can't get money already spent or time invested back. Exit point criteria will help you identify sunk costs and hopefully keep you from throwing good money after bad.

Law #10 - The reward at the end of a failed risk

Even if a project is deemed a failure either because it was scrapped or its ROI ended up significantly below expectations, there is still value to be realized. A thorough post mortem should be conducted to isolate the reason(s) for the failure.

Once the failure point is identified, it should be chalked up as a lesson learned exercise so that the errors that caused the failure will not happen again in the future. Remedial action should be undertaken to alleviate the possibility of repeated mistakes.

Remedial actions may involve additional training for employees, changes to drawings or specifications, reexamination of suppliers for the materials or equipment involved or a change to standard operating procedures (SOP). In the worst case scenario, if the culprit is an incompetent worker or subcontractor, termination may be the best solution.

Law #11 — If at first you don't succeed, try and try again

In the Walt Disney animated movie "Meet the Robinsons", there is one of my favorite scenes from all kids' movies. The main character is a little boy who loves inventions.

The little boy tries something and fails. Expecting criticism, he was surprised when his friends and family basically threw a party. "Congratulations! You failed!" They were excited for him. He was massively confused, but they reminded him that this failure means he was one step closer to success.

I wish I had this attitude in my own risk taking. I met a man one time who was excited to tell me about a business venture he was starting. "I don't know if this one will be the big one, or if it will be the next one... but one day I will succeed. And I won't stop until I get there."

His words have stuck with me over the years. I have seen him try, and fail, many times. But he isn't giving up. Truthfully, he hasn't made it yet. But I have no doubt that he will.

In the wise words of Thomas Edison, "I have not failed. I've just found 10,000 ways that won't work.

THE RISK IQ TEST: FINAL EXAM

As I promised earlier, here is another run at the Risk IQ test now that you have finished the book. By the way, don't forget the appendices. I have some more good information back there.

For each of the questions below, simply mark a YES or NO. At the bottom, you'll simply tally up the YES column and the NO column and plug those numbers into the simple formula provided.

PERSONAL RISK IQ

Risk Basics
- Y N - I understand the definition for risk management.
- Y N - I understand what a risk assessment is.
- Y N - I understand what a vulnerability is.
- Y N - I understand what probability is.
- Y N - I understand what impact is.
- Y N - I understand what compensating controls are.
- Y N - I understand what an inherent risk is.
- Y N - I understand what a residual risk is.
- Y N - I understand how to weigh the pros and cons of a risk-based decision.
- Y N - I understand the difference between and benefits of retaining, avoiding, reducing and transferring a risk.

Y N - I understand Total Cost of Risk.

Y N - I understand what property insurance is.

Y N - I understand what liability insurance is.

Y N - I understand what a declarations page is.

Y N - I understand what an exclusion is.

Y N - I understand what an endorsement is.

Y N - I understand the difference between "named perils" and "specific perils".

Personal Risks

Y N - I have performed a personal risk assessment on my life.

Y N - I understand health insurance and have made an informed decision on how to proceed.

Y N - I understand ancillary insurances (dental, vision) and have made an informed decision on how to proceed.

Y N - I understand home insurance/rental insurance and have made an informed decision on how to proceed.

Y N - I understand personal liability insurance and have made an informed decision on how to proceed.

Y N - I have performed a housing vulnerability check and implemented necessary changes.

Y N - I have performed a vehicular vulnerability check and implemented necessary changes.

Y N - I understand risks I encounter while traveling and implement the necessary precautions when necessary.

Y N - I understand cyber risks and have implemented the necessary precautions/protections.

Financial Risks

Y N - I have three months of savings in the bank in case of an emergency.

Y N - I have a retirement account set up.

Y N - I understand identity protection and have made an informed decision on how to proceed.

Y N - I understand what ransomeware is and how to protect my data against compromise

End of Life Risks

Y N - I understand and have evaluated life insurance and have made an informed decision on how to proceed.

Y N - I have created a last will and testament.

End of Personal Risk IQ test

Risk IQ Formula

Count the number of YES answers and the number of NO answers. Divide the number of No answers by the number of YES answers. Multiply that number by 100.

Your answer will be between 1 and 100, with 100 being a perfect score.

Your Personal Risk IQ Score _____

BUSINESS RISK IQ

Risk Basics

- Y N - I understand the definition of risk management.
- Y N - I understand what a risk assessment is.
- Y N - I understand what a vulnerability is.
- Y N - I understand what probability is.
- Y N - I understand what impact is.
- Y N - I understand what compensating controls are.
- Y N - I understand what an inherent risk is.
- Y N - I understand what a residual risk is.
- Y N - I understand how to weigh the pros and cons of a risk-based decision.
- Y N - I understand Total Cost of Risk.
- Y N - I understand the difference between and benefits of retaining, avoiding, reducing and transferring a risk.
- Y N - I understand what property insurance is.
- Y N - I understand what liability insurance is.
- Y N - I understand what a declarations page is.
- Y N - I understand what an exclusion is.
- Y N - I understand what an endorsement is.
- Y N - I understand the difference between "named perils" and "specific perils".
- Y N - I understand a workers compensation policy and how I can control the costs.

Y N - I understand what crime insurance is.

Y N - I understand what errors and omissions insurance is.

Y N - I understand what directors' and officers' liability insurance is.

Y N - I understand what errors and omissions insurance is.

Y N - I understand property insurance.

Y N - I understand liability insurance.

Y N - I understand what health insurance options I have for my company.

Y N - I understand Business Interruption Insurance and Contingent Business Interruption Insurance.

Commercial Risks

Y N - I have performed a commercial risk assessment on my business.

Y N - I have made an informed choice about choosing an insurance broker.

Y N - I have performed a safety audit at my place of business.

Y N - I have performed a vehicular vulnerability check and implemented necessary safeguards.

Y N - I have created and implemented a business continuity plan for my pace of business.

Y N - I understand cyber risks and have implemented the necessary precautions/protections.

Y N - I understand active shooter risks and have made a plan for my place of business.

Y N - I have researched the best available safety equipment and have made an informed decision on how to proceed.

Y N - I have contacted a disaster recovery company and have established a relationship that will guarantee services within 24 hours in the case of an emergency.

Y N - I implement employee trainings on a regular basis.

Y N - I have policies in place to back up data on a regular basis.

Business Continuation Risks

Y N - I understand what a business continuity plan is.

Y N - I understand and have evaluated life insurance and have made an informed decision on how to proceed.

Y N - I have created a last will and testament that clearly outlines my instructions for my company in the event of my death or incapacitation.

Y N - I have evaluated a buy-sell agreement or key man insurance policy.

End of Business Risk IQ test

APPENDIX A:
Questions to ponder

Your Risk Personality Type equates to your overall posture concerning risk. It corresponds to a personality type (Risk Seeker, Risk Taker, Risk Neutral, Risk Hesitant, and Risk Avoider). You will best determine your Risk Personality type by reading the descriptions of each. To help give you a better idea of your risk tendencies, I put together a list of questions to help you assess your openness or aversion to risk.

Likelihood of Behaviors

When you think of the word "risk," how likely are you to equate it to danger?

- *The higher the likelihood, the more of a risk avoider you are.*

When you think of the word "risk," how likely are you to equate it to uncertainty?

- *The higher the likelihood, the more of a risk neutral or risk hesitant person you are.*

When you think of the word "risk," how likely are you to equate it to opportunity?

- *The higher the likelihood, the more of a risk taker or risk seeker you are.*

How likely are you to not bother fastening your seat belt when only driving a few blocks to the store?
- *The higher the likelihood, the more of a risk taker or risk seeker you are.*

Let's say you're running just a little late on your way to work, how likely are you to speed up and break the speed limit to get there on time?
- *The higher the likelihood, the more of a risk taker or risk seeker you are.*

When buying car insurance, how likely are you to choose a low deductible even if the rate is significantly higher?
- *The higher the likelihood, the more of a risk avoider you are.*

When going on an expensive vacation, how likely are you to purchase trip insurance assuming that insurance costs 10% of what you paid for the travel itself?
- *The higher the likelihood, the more of a risk avoider you are.*

How likely are you to purchase a home security system?
- *The higher the likelihood, the more of a risk avoider you are.*

Let's say you're buying a kitchen appliance in the $100-$200 price range, how likely are you to pay $10-$20 extra for the extended warranty?
- *The higher the likelihood, the more of a risk avoider you are.*

When you're ready to invest money, how likely are you to choose annuities with guaranteed returns over other securities currently offering higher return rates?

- *The higher the likelihood, the more of a risk avoider you are.*

Assuming you have money you're ready to invest in the stock market, how likely are you to choose blue chip stocks over the stock of companies many experts are predicting to show above-average earnings this year?

- *The higher the likelihood, the more of a risk hesitant person or risk avoider you are.*

When faced with a major financial decision, would you be more worried about a possible loss or more optimistic about a potential gain?

- *The higher the likelihood, the more of a risk hesitant person or risk avoider you are.*

When buying a new home, how likely are you to choose an ARM (Adjustable Rate Mortgage) over a fixed rate mortgage?

- *The higher the likelihood, the more of a risk taker or risk seeker you are.*

Assume you had an initial investment portfolio with substantial net worth. If it dropped significantly in value in a month, how likely would you be to convert your investments to cash?

- *The higher the likelihood, the more of a risk hesitant person or risk avoider you are.*

Comfort Level With Given Scenarios

Let's say you're offered a job with a promising start-up company with an attractive signing bonus and stock options. How comfortable would you be quitting your existing job with the stable company where you're currently employed?

- *The more comfortable you are, the more of a risk taker or risk seeker you are.*

Your current company is laying people off and they have offered you a severance package and a position as an independent consultant with them at a higher rate of pay than you had been earning but no benefits. You know there are other companies in the area that are hiring employees with your skill set. How comfortable would you be accepting the offer of the consultant job?

- *The more comfortable you are, the more of a risk taker or risk seeker you are.*

Assuming you feel pretty confident in your salesmanship capabilities, how comfortable would you be in accepting a job offer with a small base pay but a lucrative commission package as opposed to a similar position with a salary equal to half the expected income potential of the commissioned job?

- *The more comfortable you are, the more of a risk taker or risk seeker you are.*

Let's say you have a great idea for a new product or service, how comfortable would you feel quitting your job and starting your own business?

- *The more comfortable you are, the more of a risk taker or risk seeker you are.*

Several friends are planning on signing up for an adventure trip involving dangerous but probably not life-threatening activities. How comfortable would you be saying no and sticking to your guns?

- *The more comfortable you are, the more of a risk hesitant person or risk avoider you are.*

APPENDIX B:
Insurance Terms

Actual Cash Value

The fair market value of a damaged, destroyed or stolen piece of property at the time of the loss. For residences, it is determined by real estate comparable values in the area. For businesses, it's generally determined by real estate brokers who value a business on cash flow and profitability. For vehicles, it's the average of recent sales amounts of vehicles of comparable year, make and model. As a general statement it is replacement costs less depreciation.

Actuary

A business professional who analyzes probabilities of risk and risk management including calculation of premiums, dividends and other applicable insurance industry standards.

Adjuster

A person who investigates claims and recommends settlement options based on estimates of damage and insurance policies coverage forms.

Agent, Insurance

An individual or business licensed by the state to sell insurance for or on behalf of an insurance company.

Aircraft Insurance

Coverage against losses involving an aircraft regarding the ownership, use or maintenance of said aircraft. Most policies even cover negligent use of an aircraft by the responsible party.

Assigned Risk

A governmental pool established to write business declined by carriers in the standard insurance market.

Binder

Temporary insurance coverage providing coverage until a policy can be written and executed. A typical example is an insured driver who purchases a new vehicle.

Bodily Injury

Physical injury to a person or persons resulting from an accidental, unintentional or even negligent act of an insured individual or company.

Book Value

Property value stated in the company's accounting system. Will typically include capitalized acquisition costs and accumulated depreciation, unamortized premium and discount, deferred origination and commitment fees, direct write-downs, and increase/decrease by adjustment.

Broker

An individual or company that represents multiple insurance companies and assists insurance buyers in selecting the policy that best fits their needs.

Burglary

Coverage against damage or theft of property resulting from criminal activity involving unauthorized entry into premises.

Cancellation

Retraction of an insurance policy before its expiration date.

Captive Agent

An insurance agent who sells or services insurance contracts for a specific insurer. A captive agent has an exclusive agreement with an insurance as opposed to a broker who can shop all carriers to find the best deal.

Catastrophe Bond

A bond issued by an insurance company with funding tied to the company's losses from disasters, or acts of God.

Claim

Demand made to an insurance company that compensation is due for a loss incurred.

Claimant

The person or company filing the claim. This may be a third party other than the insured.

Collision (Auto)

Compensation due to the vehicle owner damage sustained to the vehicle. The damage may be due to a collision with another vehicle or moving object or to a fixed object.

Common Carrier Liability

A policy that covers transportation companies such as trucking companies, delivery services, buses and aircraft that carry goods for customers.

Comprehensive - Auto

Coverage of losses that occurred to the insured's vehicle in cases other than accidents or collisions. Typical examples may be fire, theft or vandalism.

Comprehensive Glass Insurance

Coverage for damages to glass objects, typically windows.

Concurrent Causation

A property loss incurred from two or more perils in which only one loss is covered but both are paid by the insurer due to simultaneous incident.

Conditions

Insurance policies state legally binding conditions outlining responsibilities that must be met by the parties. They are basically the "rules of engagement" governing the execution of the policy.

Decline

The act of refusing to cover a certain individual, company or peril.

Deductible

The Insured's obligation before the insurer has an obligation.

Dental Insurance

Insurance policies providing only dental treatment benefits such as routine dental examinations, preventive dental work, and dental procedures needed to treat tooth decay and diseases of the teeth and jaw. Most typical medial insurance policies do not cover dental expenses; thus a separate policy is needed.

Depreciation

A lowering of the value of an asset as it ages.

Disability Insurance

A policy that provides financial compensation for insured wage earners when they become unable to work in their current field of endeavor due to injuries or illness. It is usually temporary until the victim is deemed healthy enough to resume work.

Endorsement

An addendum to an insurance policy used to add or delete coverage for items other than what is covered by the standard policy. This can also be called a rider.

Exclusion

Perils or situations that are exclusively not covered by a policy. One case would be insurance against earthquake damage

Expiration Date

The specified ending date after which the policy is no longer in effect.

Face Amount

The financial amount due to the beneficiary(ies) when the insured person dies.

Financial Guarantee Insurance

An insurance policy, surety bond, or indemnity contract that guarantees financial compensation will be paid to the claimant or obligee when another party fails to meet its obligation to the insured party. The most common case is when the third party fails to perform as a contract stipulates whether it be for goods or services. .

Fire Insurance

A policy which covers the insured against damages to real and/or personal property due to a fire.

Fronting

An arrangement in which a primary insurer acts as the insurer of record by issuing a policy, but then passes the entire risk to a reinsurer in exchange for a commission.

Good Driver Discount

A premium discount given to "good drivers," typically defined as operators of vehicles who have had their covered vehicle for at least three years without having a point charged against their driving record and have not been at fault in an accident causing bodily injury or death to another person. This good driver test applies to all drivers in the household of the insured.

Grace Period

A period of time which the insurance company will allow a policy to remain in force after the premium goes past due.

Guaranteed Insurability

An option granted by a life insurance company that allows an insured person to add additional coverage without the need to prove insurability.

Hazard

A circumstance which tends to increase the probability or severity of a loss.

Health Insurance

A policy reimburses insured parties for medical expenses. Policies may include deductibles, co-pays, maximum out-of-pocket clauses and many other provisions that affect the insured's participation.

Homeowner's Insurance

A policy purchased by a home owner to cover perils that may cause destruction of or damage to a personal residence. Typical coverage includes incidents of fire, burglary, vandalism and such.

Incontestable Clause

A provision in a policy in which the insured agrees not to challenge the policy's validity after a stated period of time.

Indemnity

An accepted legal principle related to insurance that holds that the individual covered by an insurance policy should be restored to the approximate financial position he or she was in prior to the loss.

Insured

The individual or company that purchased the policy and will receive financial compensation in case of a loss. This does not apply to surety bonds where the person purchasing the bond is insuring a third party.

Insurer

The insurance company issuing the policy.

Key-Man Insurance

Life insurance covering key persons in a business—man or woman. These are people whose death would seriously impair operation of the business. The business pays for the policy and is the beneficiary.

Lapse

Termination of a policy due to failure to pay the required renewal premium.

Legal Insurance

An insurance policy that essentially prepays attorney fees in cases of claims made against the insured.

Liability - Auto

An automobile insurance policy that covers the policyholder's legal liability when another party is injured or sustains property damage in an accident deemed to be the fault of the insured.

Liability Insurance

Protection for claims filed against the insured party for compensation in cases of bodily injury, property damage, errors, omissions, or cyber-attack where the named insured is negligent. There are liability policies that cover policyholders for a wide array of damages such as errors & omissions insurance for professional workers and company executives.

Life Insurance

A policy that will pay a specific financial amount to beneficiaries upon the death of the insured party.

Limit

Maximum amount of money an insurer will pay either in total or for specific coverage areas.

Loan Value

The amount of money that can be borrowed by a policyholder who pledges the value of the policy as collateral.

Machinery Insurance

Covers losses resulting from destruction, damage or malfunction of industrial machinery. Such losses are typically not covered by property insurance policies and thus the need for a separate policy covering equipment and machinery.

Marine Insurance

Any property that needs coverage due to mobility of property. Typically for transportation ships and barges carrying goods. In some cases, marine insurance is extended to also cover land and air transport.

Material Misrepresentation

A violation committed when a policyholder or one applying for a policy makes a false statement.

Medical Payments

Policies are to pay expenses for medical services and /or funeral costs when bodily injury or death is caused by an accident. Usually the insured does not need to be negligent for payments to be made.

Medicare Advantage Plan

An HMO, PPO, or Private Fee-For Service Plan that contracts with Medicare Advantage Prescription Drug Plan also includes drug benefits. The plan may provide extra coverage such as vision, hearing, dental, and/or health and wellness programs. Medicare pays a fixed amount for insured's care every month to the companies offering Medicare Advantage plans.

Medicare Part D

Stand-Alone coverage written through individual contracts; stand-alone Part D coverage written through group contracts and certificates; and Part D coverage written on employer groups where the reporting entity is responsible for reporting claims to the Centers for Medicare & Medicaid Services (CMS).

Misquote

An incorrect statement or estimate involving an insurance premium.

Mortgage Insurance

A policy which pays off a mortgage when the insured dies.

Mutual Insurance Company

An insurance company organized as a mutual fund and owning a capital stock insurer or insurers for the benefit of pooling risk for many people, typically those in the same industry.

Optional Coverages

Coverages that are not included in a base standard policy but may be added for an additional fee. For instance, if replacement cost coverage is not included in your policy automatically, it may be available as an optional coverage.

Peril

Any destructive or damaging event that causes a financial loss, such as a fire or robbery.

Policy Limit

The maximum monetary funds a policy will pay out, either in total or for specific situations stated in the policy.

Premium

The monetary fee charged by an insurance company for a policy.

Premium Financing

A loan extended by a financial institution to an insured to pay the premiums on a policy.

Pro-Rata Cancellation

If an insurance company cancels a policy before its stated end date, the total premium for the partial year is calculated as a prorated amount based on the start and cancellation dates.

Property Damage

Material damage done to a third party's property by accidental, intentional or negligence of the insured.

Quote

An estimate of an insurance policy premium cost based on information provided by the party applying for the insurance.

Replacement Cost

The cost to replace an insured item at current market value. The compensation is not reduced by subtracting depreciation costs from the original cost of the item.

Reinstatement

The restoration of a policy that has lapsed. Most companies require that past due premium payments be made for reinstatement to occur.

Rider

Also called an endorsement, a rider is an addendum to a policy, typically to add coverage.

Self-Insurance

Type of insurance often used for high frequency low severity risks where risk is not transferred to an insurance company but retained and accounted for internally.

Short-Rate Cancellation

This may apply in situations where the policyholder cancels the policy. With short-rate cancellation, the insurer is entitled to retain a greater percentage of unearned premium (UEP) than would otherwise be retained with pro rata cancellation.

Special Form

Previously called "all risk". This broad property form includes coverages for all perils that are not excluded.

Sprinkler Insurance

Covers property damage caused by water accidentally discharged from an automatic sprinkler system.

Subrogation

A situation where an insurer, on behalf of the insured, has a legal right to bring a liability suit against a third party who caused losses to the insured.

Surcharge

An additional fee charged by insurance company. On auto policies, for instance, it could be an extra charge for undue traffic violations.

Term Life Insurance

A life insurance policy that pays a benefit in the event of the death of the insured during a specified term.

Title Insurance

Covers a real estate buyer if during the closing process for financial losses if the title is not free and clear of defects previously unknown.

Underwriting

Insurance underwriters evaluate the risk and exposures of those applying for insurance coverage. They determine the amount of coverage a given applicant can receive, how much they should pay for it, or whether even to accept the risk and insure them. Most states, however, only provide bodily injury coverage. Also, states that do provide property damage often have a limit- often around $2500.

Uninsured Motorist Coverage

The insurance company compensates you and your passengers for bodily injuries caused by an uninsured motorist or a hit-and-run driver.

Universal Life Insurance

Adjustable life insurance under which premiums and coverage are adjustable, company expenses are not specifically disclosed to the insured but a financial report is provided to policyholder's annually.

Waiting Period

A period of time set forth in an insurance policy which must end before coverages begin.

Whole Life Insurance

A life insurance policy that pays benefits upon the death of the insured and also accumulates a cash value.

Workers Compensation Insurance

Coverage providing benefits to employees for job-related injuries regardless of who was at fault. Coverage includes medical care, death, disability, and rehabilitation. Workers Comp coverages are mandated by state laws.

APPENDIX C:
Risk Tolerance Study

Investment Risk Tolerance - Individuals

For the subject of risk tolerance, I went to one of the top experts in the field—a firm called FinaMetrica. The company provides assistance and advice in the area of financial planning. This information is very similar to our Risk Personality Profiles. FinaMetrica provides an evidence based look at risk tolerance in another light.

Since the FinaMetrica study was performed using their in-depth survey questions and their findings are presented here in narrative form, you'll find a good bit of repetitive verbiage in their findings. Please focus on the numbers and numerical ranges in the text rather than the verbiage repeated from each of the questions.

The FinaMetrica Risk Tolerance Toolkit measures risk tolerance on a scale of 0 to 100. To make the scores and reports more meaningful, the scale has been divided into seven segments called Risk Groups.

Below is a bell chart showing graphically how the seven groups are delineated:

Risk Group	1	2	3	4	5	6	7
Score Range	Less than 25	25-34	35-44	45-54	55-64	65-74	75 or more
Number in Group	1%	6%	24%	38%	24%	6%	1%

1. Extremely low risk taker.
2. Very low risk taker.
3. Low risk taker.
4. Average risk taker.
5. High risk taker
6. Very high risk taker.
7. Extremely high risk taker

The Risk Group descriptions itemized below were devised from a questionnaire answered by all participants in the sample group who responded to the FinaMetrica Risk Tolerance survey. The twenty five questions considered in the analysis were selected on the basis of their utility in providing a general understanding of the Risk Groups. To help you determine your Risk IQ profile, use the descriptions of each group to identify the one that best fits your feeling where financial risks are involved.

Risk Group 1 - Extremely low risk takers

They think of risk as danger and are prepared to take only a very small degree of risk with their financial decisions. They have, at most, little confidence in their ability to make good financial decisions and usually feel at least somewhat pessimistic about their major decisions after they make them.

When faced with a major financial decision they are always more concerned about the possible losses than the possible gains. They would definitely choose more job security with a small pay increase rather than less job security with a big pay increase.

When things go wrong financially they adapt very uneasily with a high degree of worry.

They have taken only a very small degree of risk with their past financial decisions and have never borrowed money to make an investment. They have never invested a large sum of money in a risky investment mainly for the "thrill" of seeing whether it went up or down in value.

It is much more important that the value of their investments does not fall than that it retains its purchasing power. Any fall in the total value of their investments would make them feel uncomfortable. In recent years, their personal investment changes have mostly or always been towards lower risk, more likely always. Over ten years they expect an investment portfolio to earn, on average, about one to one and a half times the rate from term deposits.

If they were borrowing a large sum of money at a time when it was not clear which way interest rates were going to move and when the fixed interest rate was 1% more than the variable rate, they would choose to have 100% of the loan at fixed interest.

Concerning government benefits and tax advantages - If there was any chance they could finish up worse off than if they had done nothing, they would not take a risk in arranging their affairs to qualify for a government benefit or obtain a tax advantage.

Risk Group 2 - Very low risk taker

They think of "risk" as "danger" or "uncertainty" and are prepared to take only a very small to small degree of risk with their financial decisions. They have little to a reasonable amount of confidence in their ability to make good financial decisions and usually feel either somewhat pessimistic or cautiously optimistic about their major decisions after they make them.

When faced with a major financial decision they are most often concerned about the possible losses than optimistic about the possible gains. Most would definitely choose more job security with a small pay increase rather than less job security with a big pay increase.

When things go wrong financially they adapt somewhat uneasily with a moderate level of trepidation.

They have taken only a very small to small degree of risk with their past financial decisions and have never borrowed money to make an investment. They have never invested a large sum of money in a risky investment mainly for the "thrill" of seeing whether it went up or down in value.

It is somewhat more important that the value of their investments does not fall than that it retains its purchasing power. For most in this category, any fall in the total value of their investments would make them feel uncomfortable, but for some a 10% drop would be tolerable. In recent years, their personal investment changes have mostly or always been towards lower risk.

Over ten years they expect an investment portfolio to earn, on average, about one and a half to two times the rate from term deposits, with one and a half times being the most common expectation.

If they were borrowing a large sum of money at a time when it was not clear which way interest rates were going to move and when the fixed interest rate was 1% more than the variable rate, they would choose to have 75%-100% of the loan at fixed interest, but generally closer to the 100% end.

Concerning government benefits and tax advantages - If there was any chance they could finish up worse off than if they had done nothing, most would not take a risk in arranging their affairs to qualify for a government benefit or obtain a tax advantage but some would take a small risk.

Risk Group 3 - Low risk taker

They think of "risk" as "uncertainty" and are prepared to take a small to medium degree of risk with their financial decisions. With small being the most likely choice. They have, at most, only a reasonable amount of confidence in their ability to make good financial decisions but usually feel somewhat optimistic about their major decisions after they make them.

When faced with a major financial decision they are usually more concerned about the possible losses than the possible gains. Most would probably choose more job security with a small pay increase rather than less job security with a big pay increase but others would definitely make that choice.

They have taken a small to medium degree of risk with their past financial decisions, more likely small, and have never borrowed money to make an investment. They have never invested a large sum of money in a risky investment mainly for the "thrill" of seeing whether it went up or down in value.

For some, it is somewhat more important that the value of their investments does not fall than that it retains its purchasing power, but for most retaining purchasing power is the more important of the two. For some, a fall of 10% in the total value of their investments would make them feel uncomfortable but for others it would take a fall of 20%.

In recent years, their personal investment changes have mostly been towards lower risk. Over ten years they expect an investment portfolio to earn, on average, about one and a half to two times the rate from term deposits, with two time being the most common expectation.

If they were borrowing a large sum of money at a time when it was not clear which way interest rates were going to move and when the fixed interest rate was 1% more than the variable rate, they would choose to have at least 50% of the loan at fixed interest.

Concerning government benefits and tax advantages - so long as there was only a small chance they could finish up worse off than if they had done nothing, most would take a risk in arranging their affairs to qualify for a government benefit or obtain a tax advantage but the minority would not take any risk.

Risk Group 4 - Average risk taker

They think of "risk" as "uncertainty" and are prepared to take a medium degree of risk with their financial decisions. They have a reasonable amount of confidence in their ability to make good financial decisions and usually feel somewhat optimistic about their major decisions after they make them.

When faced with a major financial decision, it's about a 50-50 split between those who are more concerned about the possible losses and those who are more optimistic about the possible gains. They would be slightly more likely to choose more job security with a small pay increase than less job security with a big pay increase.

They have taken a small to medium degree of risk with their past financial decisions, more likely medium, and most have never borrowed money to make an investment. They have never invested a large sum of money in a risky investment primarily for the excitement of seeing whether it went up or down in value.

It is somewhat more important that the value of their investments retains its purchasing power than that it does not fall. For most, a fall of 20% in the total value of their investments would make them feel uncomfortable but for others it would take a 33% fall.

In recent years, for most there have been no changes in the risk of their personal investments but for those that have changed, the changes have been mostly towards lower risk. Over ten years they expect an investment portfolio to earn, on average, about two to two and a half times the rate offered for term deposits, with two times being the most common expectation.

If they were borrowing a large sum of money at a time when it was not clear which way interest rates were going to move and when the fixed interest rate was 1% more than the variable rate, most would choose to have 50% of the loan at fixed interest but some would choose 75%-100%.

Concerning government benefits and tax advantages; so long as there was only a small chance they could finish up worse off than if they had done nothing, they would take a risk in arranging their affairs to qualify for a government benefit or obtain a tax advantage

Risk Group 5 - High risk taker

They think of "risk" as "uncertainty" or "opportunity" and are prepared to take a medium degree of risk with their financial decisions. Most have a reasonable amount of confidence in their ability to make good financial decisions and some have a great deal of confidence. They usually feel somewhat optimistic about their major decisions after they make them.

When faced with a major financial decision they are usually more concerned about the possible gains. They would be slightly more likely to choose less job security with a big pay increase than more job security with a small pay increase.

When things go wrong financially, while some adapt somewhat uneasily but most adapt with relevant ease.

They have taken a medium degree of risk with their past financial decisions and almost half have borrowed money to make an investment. Most have never invested a large sum of money in a risky investment just for the excitement of seeing whether it went up or down in value.

It is somewhat more important that the value of their investments retains its purchasing power than that it does not fall. For some, a fall of 20% in the total value of their investments would make them feel uncomfortable but for most it would take a 33% fall.

In recent years, for most there have been no changes in the risk of their personal investments but for those that have changed, the changes have been mostly towards higher risk. Over ten years, most expect an investment portfolio to earn more than three times the rate of term deposits, most likely three or more times.

If they were borrowing a large sum of money at a time when it was not clear which way interest rates were going to move and when the fixed interest rate was 1% more than the variable rate, most would choose to have 50% of the loan at fixed interest but some would choose 75%-100%.

Concerning government benefits and tax advantages - most would take a risk in arranging their affairs to qualify for a government benefit or obtain a tax advantage so long as there was only a small chance they could finish up worse off than if they had done nothing. However some would take a risk if there was a better than 50% chance of finishing up better off.

Risk Group 6 - Very high risk taker

They think of "risk" as "opportunity" and are prepared to take a medium to large degree of risk with their financial decisions, more likely large than medium. Most have a great deal of confidence in their ability to make good financial decisions but some have only a reasonable amount. They usually feel somewhat or very optimistic about their major decisions after they make them.

When faced with a major financial decision they are usually more concerned about the possible gains. Most would probably choose less job security with a big pay increase rather than more job security with a small pay increase.

When things go wrong financially they adapt somewhat easily.

They have taken a medium to large degree of risk with their past financial decisions, more likely large, and half have borrowed money to make an investment. Most have invested a large sum of money in a risky investment mainly for the "thrill" of seeing whether it went up or down in value, but not very frequently.

It is somewhat to much more important that the value of their investments retains its purchasing power than that it does not fall, more likely much more important. For most a fall of 33% in the total value of their investments would make them feel uncomfortable but for some it would take a 50% fall.

In recent years, their personal investment changes have mostly been towards higher risk. Over ten years they expect an investment portfolio to earn, on average, at least three times the rate from term deposits.

If they were borrowing a large sum of money at a time when it was not clear which way interest rates were going to move and when the fixed interest rate was 1% more than the variable rate, most would choose to have 50% of the loan at variable interest but some would choose 75%-100%.

Concerning government benefits and tax advantages - most would take a risk in arranging their affairs to qualify for a government benefit or obtain a tax advantage if there was a better than 50% chance they could finish up better off than if they had done nothing. However some would only take a risk if there was only a small chance of finishing up worse off.

Risk Group 7 - Extremely high risk taker

They think of risk as an opportunity and are prepared to take a large to very large degree of risk with their financial decisions. Most have a great deal of confidence in their ability to make good financial decisions and some have complete confidence. They usually feel very optimistic about their major decisions after they make them.

When faced with a major financial decision they are usually, if not always, more concerned about the possible gains. Most would definitely choose less job security with a big pay increase than more job security with a small pay increase.

When things go wrong financially they adapt fairly easily.

They have taken a large to very large degree of risk with their past financial decisions. They have borrowed money to make an investment. Most have invested a large sum of money in a risky investment mainly for the "thrill" of seeing whether it went up or down in value.

It is much more important that the value of their investments retains its purchasing power than that it does not fall. For some, a fall of 50% in the total value of their investments would make them feel uncomfortable but for others it would take a fall of more than 50%. In recent years, their personal investment changes have mostly or always been towards higher risk. Over ten years they expect an investment portfolio to earn, on average, more than three times the rate of term deposits.

If they were borrowing a large sum of money at a time when it was not clear which way interest rates were going to move and when the fixed interest rate was 1% more than the variable rate, most would choose to have 100% of the loan at variable interest but some would choose 75%.

Concerning government benefits and tax advantages - they would take a risk in arranging their affairs to qualify for a government benefit or obtain a tax advantage if there was a better than 50% chance they could finish up better off than if they had done nothing.

Below is a chart showing the average spread of the investment portfolio for each of the sevens groups:

Portfolio	Mix of Investment in Portfolio		
	High Risk/Return	Medium Risk/Return	Low Risk/Return
1	0%	0%	100%
2	0%	30%	70%
3	10%	40%	50%
4	30%	40%	30%
5	50%	40%	10%
6	70%	30%	0%
7	100%	0%	0%

The above analysis was provided by FinaMetrica Corporation from their study on personal risk tolerance

Risk Tolerance - Business

Financial Investments

tart-up and early-stage businesses of course are investing most of their available funds into their own companies. Even when they start making profits, those profits are almost always invested right back into the venture.

For companies fortunate enough to have made it over the early hurdles into steady profitability and cash flow, they'd rather not let any excess cash sit idle on their balance sheets. Investing that extra cash for interest income or capital gains is part of the company's treasury function.

Whether it's part of the treasury unit or a separate business unit of its own, most large companies have a risk management executive or department that oversees the investment activities of the company among other areas of risk. In smaller companies, the risk management responsibility may fall on the shoulders of the Chief Financial Officer (CFO) or perhaps the senior management team.

Since the economic meltdown of the 2007-2008 period, risk management has become an essential and critical practice in most organizations. It is necessary for managing uncertainty and its effect on achieving organizational objectives. Such uncertainty related to future financial outcomes either improve or impair the organization's financial position.

As a company gains experience in risk management, they develop a better understanding of both risk appetite and risk tolerance and may develop standards and guidelines for both. Since the terms "risk appetite" and "risk tolerance" are often used interchangeably, I did research to delineate the difference. There are only minor differences between the two, but they need to be understood. These are the two definitions I found to be the most appropriate:

- **Risk appetite**—This is the total exposed amount of money that an organization wishes to undertake on the basis of risk-return trade-offs for investments and major new projects. This being the case, risk appetite is tightly linked to targeted return rates. Risk appetite guidelines may be expressed qualitatively or quantitatively or a combination of the two. They may be applied to either individual risks or as an aggregation. In general, risk appetite refers to the amount that an organization is willing to put at risk actively for ventures in the quest for financial rewards. These rewards are tightly tied to the firm's goals and objectives.

- **Risk tolerance** is the amount of uncertainty an organization is prepared to accept either in aggregate, by business unit, by project or by risk category. Rather than looking solely at the total amount of money an organization is willing to put at risk, the tolerance for risk is more about setting boundaries, which can be in terms of cost, interference with company objectives or negative impact on the firm's reputation. Boundaries are often set for both upper and lower thresholds. Not taking enough risks may result in missed opportunities while risking too much may put the company's financial health in danger. Risk tolerance is also highly dependent on how well capitalized the organization is. The deeper the pockets, the more can be put at risk.

Another term often heard when the conversation about risk come up is risk culture. Each organization has its own risk culture. Using risk appetite and risk tolerance as a base, risk culture also involves norms and traditions existing in the organization. Behaviors of departments, groups and individuals establish the manner in which risks are perceived and handled.

Decisions made by individuals who fail to understand the company's risk culture or flat out ignore it can create a great deal of trouble.

Although decisions about risk appetite and risk tolerance are normally made by an organization's executive management and board, other key stakeholders may get involved in certain circumstances. These stakeholders are typically the middle managers considered as leaders and influencers within the organization.

If the risk attitudes of executive management, the board and key stakeholders are not in alignment, problems can arise. If risk appetite and risk tolerance standards are not stated in crystal clear terms, the resulting 'wiggle room' may cause different factions to vary from the intent of the guidelines.

Risk appetite and tolerance standards can be communicated and enforced through all levels of the organization with the use of a number of tools. Written guideline documents and policy statements are at the forefront. Another might be approval and spending authorization levels. Perhaps one of the most effective is having some sort of compensation tied to the achievement of KPIs tied directly to target risk levels.

The Balancing Act

Bringing risk appetite, risk tolerance and risk culture together under a single umbrella should be seen as a delicate balancing act. An organization's board, executives and key stakeholders may have varying philosophies on how much risk should be handled. In addition to the internal philosophies and behaviors, there are also external factors that come into play. The industry or industries in which a company operates must be taken into consideration. For international corporations, the cultures, political situations and operating conditions abroad must also be taken into consideration.

Companies with higher risk appetites are typically more interested in on the possibility of a significant increase in capital valuation earnings. So it follows that they will be prone to accept above average risks to achieve those financial goals. Early-stage, high-potential, high-risk, growth companies typically lead the pack when it comes to living with greater volatility and uncertainty. They are more likely to take chances where legal and regulatory matters are concerned.

Those with lesser risk appetites are naturally more risk averse with their primary focus being on financial stability, steady growth and stable earnings. They are typically more guarded against market fluctuations and take legal and regulatory requirements more seriously than their feisty counterparts.

At the center of the balancing act might be a risk target, the desired level of risk that the organization believes is optimal to meet its objectives. Unexpected or out of tolerance deviations from the target should trigger further analysis and action. The balancing act is also affected by risk capacity, the amount of risk an organization can actually bear.

Risk/Reward Trade-Offs in Daily Operations

High level risk tolerance standards and guidelines are inconsequential if not communicated to all levels of the organization and put into practice in day-to-day operations. How these guidelines are applied to risk/reward decision making at the operational level of the business is the key to the organization's overall effectiveness and financial health.

Monitoring well-defined KPIs across all areas including finance, legal, operations, regulatory compliance, human resources and quality control is essential. Each of these individual areas must have defined levels of risk that are synchronized with the strategy, goals and objective of the overall organization as a whole.

One must take care that not all KPIs are carried down to the lowest levels of the operation. For example, let's say a target gross profit percentage target is set for a product line or group of lines. There may be individual products that fall significantly below that targeted percentage due to competitor pricing or market conditions. Eliminating certain products based solely on the numbers could actually be riskier than keeping them if they are needed to meet customer service expectations.

Real or Merely Perceived?

Oftentimes, companies get overwhelmed due to handling the large array of risk decisions that must be made. One differentiator that can sort them out is determining which are actually real and which as only perceived. To determine which is which, one must figure out whether it is relevant and essential to achieving the organization's goals. If a particular risk does not meet this litmus test, it can safely be put on the back burner side until a later date as matters change.

FinaMetrica Resource

I'd like to thank FinaMetrica, an international risk management advisory firm for allowing us to use a portion of their findings for this chapter. They have a more in-depth tool called the FinaMetrica Profiling System. For more information on their service in the US, you can reach their Atlanta, GA office at (403) 320-6047.

ABOUT THE AUTHOR

DR. AMY ARP is an entrepreneur, inventor, motivational speaker, published author, and a Commercial Lines Insurance Coverage Specialist. She graduated with honors from both Texas State University with a Masters in Social Work and from Trinity with a Doctorate in Philosophy. She is the founder of STEPS, a non-profit which helps break cycles of poverty and crisis in individuals and families.

Her background includes sales positions in multiple industries, four successful startup businesses, ten years as a COO, published author, itinerant speaker, and founder of a non-profit organization.

For speaking engagements, please contact Amy at
dramyarp@gmail.com

www.ingramcontent.com/pod-product-compliance
Lightning Source LLC
Chambersburg PA
CBHW050215230526
45470CB00001B/402